CRYPTOGRAPHY

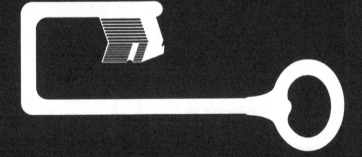

The MIT Press Essential Knowledge Series

A complete list of books in this series can be found online at
https://mitpress.mit.edu/books/series/mit-press-essential-knowledge-series.

CRYPTOGRAPHY

PANOS LOURIDAS

The MIT Press | Cambridge, Massachusetts | London, England

The MIT Press would like to thank the anonymous peer reviewers who provided comments on drafts of this book. The generous work of academic experts is essential for establishing the authority and quality of our publications. We acknowledge with gratitude the contributions of these otherwise uncredited readers.

This book was set in Chaparral Pro by New Best-set Typesetters Ltd. Printed and bound in the United States of America.

Library of Congress Cataloging-in-Publication Data

Names: Louridas, Panos, author.
Title: Cryptography / Panos Louridas.
Description: Cambridge, Massachusetts : MIT Press, [2024] | Series: The
    MIT Press essential knowledge series | Includes bibliographical references
    and index.
Identifiers: LCCN 2024002672 (print) | LCCN 2024002673 (ebook) |
    ISBN 9780262549028 (paperback) | ISBN 9780262379588 (epub) |
    ISBN 9780262379595 (pdf)
Subjects: LCSH: Cryptography. | Coding theory.
Classification: LCC QA268 .L68 2024 (print) | LCC QA268 (ebook) |
    DDC 652/.8—dc23/eng/20240326
LC record available at https://lccn.loc.gov/2024002672
LC ebook record available at https://lccn.loc.gov/2024002673

10 9 8 7 6 5 4 3 2 1

CONTENTS

SERIES FOREWORD

The MIT Press Essential Knowledge series offers accessible, concise, beautifully produced pocket-size books on topics of current interest. Written by leading thinkers, the books in this series deliver expert overviews of subjects that range from the cultural and the historical to the scientific and the technical.

In today's era of instant information gratification, we have ready access to opinions, rationalizations, and superficial descriptions. Much harder to come by is the foundational knowledge that informs a principled understanding of the world. Essential Knowledge books fill that need. Synthesizing specialized subject matter for nonspecialists and engaging critical topics through fundamentals, each of these compact volumes offers readers a point of access to complex ideas.

Our secrets make us who we are. They are what we know about ourselves and we don't want anybody else to know. We may project any persona we want against the world, choosing what to keep for ourselves. Our secrets also determine our friends and those we love from mere acquaintances and strangers. It is to our friends that we choose to share them. We trust someone when we render ourselves vulnerable to them, and we make ourselves vulnerable by sharing with them things that are sensitive and could hurt us if they fall into the wrong hands. We have a right to privacy because we have a right to keep something inside. And our need to keep things private goes beyond our personal matters. We need confidentiality in our professional lives. Businesses need to keep secrets. So do governments and armies. And all, ourselves, companies, governments, and armies, choose to share their secrets, but only to those they trust.

This book is an introduction to cryptography, the art and science of keeping and revealing secrets. That is a blithe definition, but we have enough pages ahead of us to flesh it out. Cryptography is ancient, and the methods of cryptography have changed over the centuries and are changing the moment these lines are being written. As we'll see, what cryptographers were doing in earlier times bears scant resemblance to what cryptographers are doing today. To understand their craft, we will have to visit the past, follow the path to where we are now, and see the signs pointing to where we may go tomorrow.

The story of keeping secrets runs parallel to that of breaking them. We devise methods that we believe will keep our confidences private, but others wish to go past our defenses and unveil them. It becomes a race: our adversaries, as we call them in cryptography, may get the better of us by finding methods that open up what we believed we had put under lock and key. Then we must devise new, better methods. These will be attacked in their turn. They may fall, and the race goes on and on.

In the thousands of years that this race has gone on, many things have changed. From small handwritten messages, our secrets now comprise reams of data about our everyday lives. Any form of electronic communication can be recorded. Most of our daily activities, from texting to video calls, can and should be kept secret. And that's just our personal communications. No enterprise or state could survive without cryptography. The need to keep secrets during conflicts has driven much of cryptography over the ages.

Anything that has been evolving for a long time must adapt to remain relevant. Cryptography is no exception. From an endeavor akin to puzzle solving, it has progressed to an amalgamation of solid mathematical foundations and lots of clever engineering. In the past, cryptography could be a gentleman's pastime. Now it is the playground of mathematicians, programmers, and computer engineers.

That presents us with a challenge. This is a book that aims to give the reader a wide understanding of cryptography. It is not just a history of cryptography and its applications, although we will go through its evolution in order to understand where we are today. But to really understand cryptography, it is necessary not only to know who did what when but also to understand *how cryptography actually works*. Modern cryptography is far more technical than cryptographic methods of the past, but should not be hand-waved into facile explanations. That would be a slight both to all the people who have worked hard to make cryptography what it is today and to the readers who deserve a better treatment of a subject that impacts in multiple ways their everyday lives.

This is definitely neither a mathematical treatise nor addressed to a select audience. Even though modern cryptography can be overwhelming, it is the author's strong conviction that the basic ideas can be understood based on what we have learned in high school. We can cover a lot of ground using only a few mathematical operations. Sometimes a pencil and paper may help, but we do not need to go into esoteric proofs. The reader should then know not just what cryptography is about but *what it really is*. And if we grasp the basics, then we can get an intuitive understanding of some advanced material.

Cryptography offers us a unique opportunity to discuss a spectrum of topics as straightforward as flipping characters of the alphabet to the capabilities and opportunities afforded by such technologies as quantum computers—technologies that are yet to be fully developed! It allows us to appreciate all the hidden machinery that gives us confidence to securely use our cell phones, computers, and home devices. Ironically, while every day we divulge willingly our precious moments to social media, we bristle when we become aware of the power of modern surveillance mechanisms. It is cryptography that allows us to dance this way: give out our information, on the one hand, when we want; keep it close to us when we don't.

Our way through cryptography will start with its roots. In the first chapter of the book, we will take a walk in a potted history of *classical cryptography*—that is, cryptography up to the twentieth century. It's a fascinating story and could fill (and has filled) whole books, full of colorful characters, plans hatched and foiled, stakes raised high, and challenges thrown that stood for centuries. Classical cryptography is indispensable in order to understand how we got where we are now, but we no longer use its methods, as they offer no security at all today. Something has changed, and this was the mechanization of cryptography. Once machines, then digital computers, were brought into play, the game was up. Cryptography is no longer something that humans do; it is something computers do on behalf of humans.

There are two main strands of modern cryptography, which we will explore in the second and third chapters of the book. The first of them, *symmetric cryptography*, hinges on an idea familiar from our everyday lives. To keep something secret, you lock it up and keep the key. Then to reveal the secret, you unlock it, using the same key—hence the adjective "symmetric." As our secrets are encoded in some digital format, this locking and unlocking is performed by algorithms working on data. We'll see how this is done, safeguarding our data and communications, from small text snippets to online video communications.

Once you are able to lock and unlock your secrets, you need to guard against another subtle but treacherous threat. Even if nobody is able to read your secrets, they may still be able to forge them. You send a locked secret, and an interloper, who is not able to unlock it, can substitute it with another locked secret; then there's scant solace in knowing that the original lock has not been picked or broken. We'll see how we get around this problem by using *message authentication codes*.

Unlocking a secret that is encrypted with symmetric cryptography is straightforward provided you have the key that locked it. Here comes a conundrum: It's all fine and dandy if you want to unlock your own secrets, as long as you've not lost your key. But what if you want to communicate your secret to somebody else? They will need the key to unlock it. If you send the locked secret along with the key to them, somebody could intercept both the secret and the key; everything is up for grabs. That means that you need a secure, confidential way to send the key. If you really had a way to do that, then probably you would not need to lock the secret in the first place; you would have sent the secret through the same secure way. If a secure way to send the key does not exist, then what is there to do? One could not lock the key itself because then you would need a secure way to send the key that locked the key, and this leads nowhere.

The solution to this catch-22 situation is the subject of the third chapter of the book. We'll see that it is possible to solve the *key exchange* problem and agree on a secret key with our interlocutor when our means of communication are not secure. Moreover, we can use two different keys instead of a single, secret one. We can lock our message using one key; once we do that, the message can be unlocked only by using the other key. Then we need to keep only the unlocking key secret; the locking key can be freely shared with anybody. This is *public key cryptography*, or *asymmetric cryptography*. The solution to the key exchange problem and public key cryptography really made secure digital communications possible. Daily, unobtrusively, we can communicate confidentially with parties we've never met without the need to meet in person to share secret keys. Asymmetric cryptography also gives us other possibilities beyond locking and unlocking secrets: it is the basis of digital signatures, by which we can certify the provenance of digital documents. When we put our signature in a document, we certify that *we* have acknowledged its content; equally important, it is a commitment: once we have given our digital signature, we cannot repudiate that we have acknowledged the document.

The basic operations of locking and unlocking are the foundations on which we have built cryptographic *protocols and applications*, which we adumbrate in the fourth chapter. There are umpteen cryptographic applications; by necessity, we will only see a handful of them, but this will give us an appreciation of their breadth and depth. How do we, for instance, browse the web securely?

In the final chapter of the book, we'll go through a smorgasbord of topics that are at the forefront of cryptography. These are new mathematical methods, quantum and post-quantum cryptography, the interplay of cryptography and computer security. We'll discover that far from being a settled field, cryptography is a vibrant, rapidly developing subject. It is fascinating to witness it evolving before our eyes—the challenges it meets; the mishaps, progress, and perhaps frustrations along the way.

We'll conclude by touching on ethics and cryptography, and some of the issues that arise from cryptography

Issues that arise from cryptography in the real world . . . are too important to be left to be discussed only by experts.

in the real world. These issues are too important to be left to be discussed only by experts. If readers partake even slightly of the passion of cryptographers working hard to move cryptography onward and upward, and if they reach the final page better equipped to be part of the conversation than when they started reading this book, then the book will have fulfilled its purpose.

CLASSICAL CRYPTOGRAPHY

An oeuvre becomes a classic when it stands the test of time. We return to the classics because centuries or even millennia following their conception, they can still talk to us as if they were created today. Not in this book. When we talk about "classical cryptography," we mean methods of cryptography that use pen and paper, and perhaps some mechanical aids, that have been developed in the past but are not used anymore. They could lock our secrets at one time, but not now. A secret protected by classical cryptography can be revealed in an instant with today's technology.

What does "classical cryptography" have to say to us today, then? Is it only of historical interest? It definitely has historical interest, but it is also more than that. Studying history allows us to understand how we got where we are now. In our topic, even a potted history will reward us with something more than that: a better grasp of what cryptography tries to do, the challenges it faces, and the process by which progress is made. And what a story it is! It is a story that will take us from twentieth-century Paris to Google, from the Islamic golden age to World War II, from ancient Greeks and Latin emperors to spy agencies.

In 1969, a Parisian author put out a book, *La Disparition*. It is about a group of individuals looking for a missing companion. But that is not all that is missing in this work; also missing is any word containing a symbol that is fifth from *A*. That was an amazing task, as no symbol is as common.

The author of *La Disparition* (*The Disappearance*) was Georges Perec, and the previous paragraph (did you notice?) should serve as an indication of how arduous the task of avoiding *E* is in English, as in French; it is the most frequent letter in both languages.[1]

It is not just the letter *E* that appears with a specific frequency. Limiting ourselves to English, in 1965, an article titled "Tables of Single-Letter and Digram Frequency Counts for Various Word-Length and Letter-Position Combinations" was published in the scholarly journal *Psychonomic Monograph Supplements*. Under this cryptic title, the article contained tables showing the frequency of letters and letter combinations in English words. Letters in English enjoy different degrees of popularity. In the article, we find indeed that the letter *E* is the most popular in the language, topping the character frequency rank.[2]

The character frequencies were constructed painstakingly by selecting 20,000 words from many texts and tabulating the counts for letter combinations. These were punched on cards and then fed into the card-sorting machines of the time.

The 20,000 selected words were a feat in the 1960s, but advances in technology can turn a feat into a trifle. Almost half a century later, on December 17, 2012, one of two authors of the article, Mark Mayzner, by now a retired eighty-five-year-old researcher, contacted Peter Norvig, the director of research at Google. Surely Google, with its abundant resources, could put itself to the same task and run it automatically, with a much more extensive corpus?

Norvig jumped at the occasion and indeed he used a corpus of 743,842,922,321 words, 97,565 of which were distinct. There were 3,563,505,777,820 letters in the Google corpus, and here is the table of frequencies for all the letters of the English alphabet:

Letter	Count (billions)	%	Letter	Count (billions)	%
E	445.2	12.49%	M	89.5	2.51%
T	330.5	9.28%	F	85.6	2.40%
A	286.5	8.04%	P	76.1	2.14%
O	272.3	7.64%	G	66.6	1.87%
I	269.7	7.57%	W	59.7	1.68%

Letter	Count (billions)	%	Letter	Count (billions)	%
N	257.8	7.23%	Y	59.3	1.66%
S	232.1	6.51%	B	52.9	1.48%
R	223.8	6.28%	V	37.5	1.05%
H	180.1	5.05%	K	19.3	0.54%
L	145.0	4.07%	X	8.4	0.23%
D	136.0	3.82%	J	5.7	0.16%
C	119.2	3.34%	Q	4.3	0.12%
U	97.3	2.73%	Z	3.2	0.09%

As you can see, the frequencies of letters in English, and it goes the same in other languages, are far from random. That is the result of the regularities inherent in human languages. A language is based on rules, those of phonetics, and grammar, and syntax. Different languages sound and are written differently, yet in each language, written words are not haphazard bunches of letters. Letters form words according to specific patterns. Yes, there are exceptions, but the evidence is that these over time give way to norms, as "a rule is the tombstone of a thousand exceptions."[3]

All of this means that human communication is not arbitrary. When we communicate with someone, we expect to exchange some information, which has some meaning. We use language (oral or written) to communicate information. As human languages have regularities, rules, and norms (or they would not be languages in the first place), we expect that the message we communicate will be understood by the community of speakers of the language. It is interesting how close the words "community" and "communication" are.

But sometimes we want to change the rules of the game. We want to communicate with somebody in such a way that nobody else will know what we are talking about. One way would be to create a new language, which would be comprehensible only to the interlocutors and completely unintelligible to everybody else. That is neither easy nor practical, as there should be no easy way to translate between the newfangled language and other normal languages (that is why varieties of pig Latin may have linguistic and cultural significance, but they are not useful for keeping secrets).

This leads us to *cryptography*: from the Greek "hidden writing," it means the study of methods that allow us to communicate securely in the presence of others who can intercept our communications. As they can intercept our communications, we have to make sure that what we say is unintelligible to them. The way we do that with cryptography is by changing our messages so that only our intended recipient can understand them. The process of changing a message so that it becomes unintelligible is called *encryption*. The initial message, which we want to send, is called

Cryptography: from the Greek "hidden writing," it means the study of methods that allow us to communicate securely in the presence of others who can intercept our communications.

plaintext or *cleartext*. Encryption converts it to something else, called *ciphertext*. The ciphertext can be read by others, but it cannot be understood by them. When it reaches the recipient, they can revert it back to the original plaintext and read its contents. This is called *decryption*. A well-defined way to encrypt a message is called a *cipher*. The issue then is how to encrypt and decrypt a message, how to design good ciphers, and, for the opponent, how to break them.

Transmuting a plaintext to a ciphertext that cannot be understood by anybody except the intended recipient is a challenge. It's not easy because the information that is hidden inside a message can be revealed if somebody, a code breaker, finds a way to induce it to come out. The story of cryptography is of codes and code breakers as well as better codes and more astute code breakers. And as we'll see, in this story, letter counting like we described plays a major role.

Simple Ciphers

Cryptography has been with us since ancient times.[4] According to Plutarch (46 CE–119 CE), the ancient Spartans used a tool called a "scytale" or "skytale" (from the Greek σκυτάλη, meaning baton or cylinder), a rod around which is wound a strip of leather or parchment. The message is

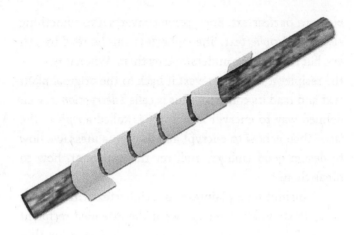

Figure 1

written across the length of the cylinder when the strip is wound on the scytale, as you can see in figure 1.[5]

When the strip is unwound, the letters on it do not make sense; you have to wind it on the scytale again so that they align correctly and the message can be read. For instance, suppose that you want to send the message "CROSS THE BRIDGE AT DAWN." You wrap the strip around the scytale and write the message as shown below in four steps, rotating the scytale by ninety degrees between each step, as in figure 2.

Then you send the strip, but not the scytale. When the messenger delivers the strip, your recipient, who must have a scytale with the same diameter, will wrap the strip around

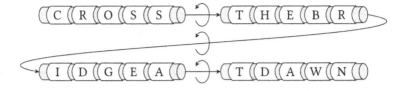

Figure 2

it and read the message. Without the scytale, though, the message reads "CTITRHDDOEGASBEWSRAN."

All that said, we are not sure that the scytale was really used by the Spartans as a cryptographic device. Plutarch wrote his account several centuries after the reported events, so he may have reported fabulations.[6] Even if the place of the scytale in cryptographic history is doubtful, it is still relevant today because it introduces us to the most straightforward code-breaking method. In our example, "CTITRHDDOEGASBEWSRAN" does not make sense, but if you know that it is supposed to be read using a scytale, you need only to try out rods of different sizes until the message is revealed. This is a case of the *brute-force* method for breaking a code. You do not apply any intelligence at all, you only try different possible solutions to your problem until you hit on the right one. You should have to resort to literal brute force here, as you would need to carve out a number of scytalae from pieces of wood. Brute force is usually our last resort because it requires a lot of effort

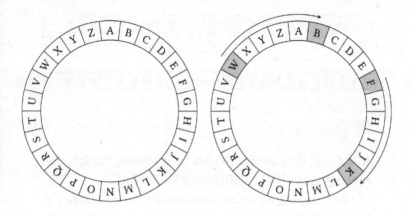

Figure 3

(probably not carving)—in fact, so much effort that it may not work at all in practice. Then we have to put our brains to work, and code breakers have come up and keep coming up with ingenious ways to break cryptographic methods.

Another old form of cryptography takes a message and changes it in the following way: take every letter in the message, and in its place put the letter that we find by moving a certain number of places forward or backward in the alphabet. If this gets us to either end of the alphabet, we just wrap around it. This is easier to see if you visualize the alphabet put on the circumference of a circle, as you can see on the left of figure 3.

Then, if you decide to shift every character, say, five places forward, the shift will be clockwise and *F* will go to

K and *W* will go to *B*, as you can see on the right of figure 3. For a backward shift, you work counterclockwise.

This method for encrypting messages is called the Caesar cipher, named after Julius Caesar. According to the historian Suetonius,

> If he had anything confidential to say, he wrote it in cipher, that is, by so changing the order of the letters of the alphabet, that not a word could be made out. If anyone wishes to decipher these, and get at their meaning, he must substitute the fourth letter of the alphabet, namely D, for A, and so with the others.[7]

This is a *substitution cipher*, meaning that it works by substituting each letter of the alphabet with another one. The rule of substitution is the shift we do along the alphabet. To decipher a ciphertext encrypted with the Caesar cipher, we only need to know the number of characters in the shift so that we can reverse it. We take each letter of the ciphertext and do the inverse substitution: from *D* back to *A*, and from *C* back to *Z*, for all letters in the encrypted message. If we assign numbers to the letters of the alphabet, so that *A* is number 0, *B* is number 1, and so on, until *Z* and number 25, then the Caesar cipher is straightforward to implement in a sequence of steps forming an algorithm:

1. Take the next letter of the plaintext. If there is no letter, stop.

2. Get the numerical value, say x, corresponding to the letter.

3. Calculate the sum $x + n$, where n is the number of characters to shift. Output the remainder of the division of $x + n$ by 26.

The remainder operation ensures that we stay within the limits of the alphabet. It is a useful operation, and we'll see it again and again in cryptography, so when we want the remainder of x divided by y we'll use the notation x mod y. The notation stands for *modulo*, which is what we call the remainder operator. The modulo is the basis of *modular arithmetic*. It is arithmetic with integer numbers wrapping around when reaching a certain value, the *modulus*. If this seems too Latin, or too exotic, it really isn't. It is a form of arithmetic that is already familiar to you, even though you may not know it by that name. You use it every time you do time calculations. Calculations involving hours are done modulo 12; when we reach that number, we wrap around and start from 0. Calculations involving minutes are done modulo 60; when we reach that number, we wrap around and start again from 0, as in the clock below, when we add 25 minutes to 4:40. The time will not be 4:65. We

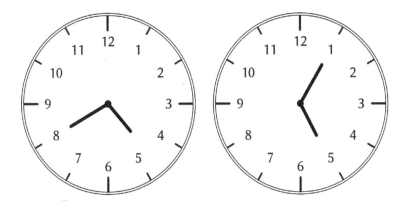

Figure 4

add the 20 minutes, get to 5:00, and then add the remaining 5 minutes to get to 5:05, as in figure 4.

Using our notation, the remainder of $x + n$ by 26 is then written $(x + n) \bmod 26$. If we go back to figure 3, the value for the character W is 22; if we add 5 to it, we get the $(22 + 5) \bmod 26 = 27 \bmod 26 = 1$, which corresponds to the letter B.

The algorithm to decrypt a message written with the Caesar cipher has almost the same steps with the encryption algorithm:

1. Take the next letter of the ciphertext. If there is no letter, stop.

2. Get the numerical value, say x, corresponding to the letter.

3. Calculate the difference $x - n$, where n is the number of characters to shift. Output the remainder of the division of $x - n$ by 26, that is, $(x - n)$ mod 26.

It may happen that $x - n$ is negative; for example, for the ciphertext letter B and a shift of 5, we have $x - n = 1 - 5 = -4$. That does not create any problem for the remainder operation because the way it is defined, -4 mod $26 = 22$.[8]
We see that to decrypt a ciphertext, we only need to know the number of positions to shift. In general, when we encrypt something, we take the plaintext and transform it in some reversible way so that the recipient of our message can later decrypt it. The piece of knowledge that the recipient must have to decrypt the message is called the *key*. In the Caesar cipher, the key is the number of characters n we use to shift.

Now suppose you intercept an encrypted message that goes like this:

YMJMFQQBFDXRJQYTKGTNQJIHFGGFLJFSITQI
WFLRFYXFYTSJJSITKNYFHTQTZWJIUTXYJWYT
TQFWLJKTWNSITTWINXUQFDMFIGJJSYFHPJIY
TYMJBFQQNYIJUNHYJIXNRUQDFSJSTWRTZXK
FHJRTWJYMFSFRJYWJBNIJYMJKFHJTKFRFSTK

```
FGTZYKTWYDKNAJBNYMFMJFADGQFHPRTZXY
FHMJFSIWZLLJIQDMFSIXTRJKJFYZWJXBNSXYT
SRFIJKTWYMJXYFNWXNYBFXSTZXJYWDNSLYM
JQNKYJAJSFYYMJGJXYTKYNRJXNYBFXXJQITRB
TWPNSLFSIFYUWJXJSYYMJJQJHYWNHHZWWJS
YBFXHZYTKKIZWNSLIFDQNLMYMTZWXNYBFXU
FWYTKYMJJHTSTRDIWNAJNSUWJUFWFYNTSK
TWMFYJBJJPYMJKQFYBFXXJAJSKQNLMYXZUF
SIBNSXYTSBMTBFXYMNWYDSNSJFSIMFIFAFWN
HTXJZQHJWFGTAJMNXWNLMYFSPQJBJSYXQTB
QDWJXYNSLXJAJWFQYNRJXTSYMJBFDTSJFHM
QFSINSLTUUTXNYJYMJQNKYXMFKYYMJUTXYJ
WBNYMYMJJSTWRTZXKFHJLFEJIKWTRYMJBFQ
QNYBFXTSJTKYMTXJUNHYZWJXBMNHMFWJXT
HTSYWNAJIYMFYYMJJDJXKTQQTBDTZFGTZYB
MJSDTZRTAJGNLGWTYMJWNXBFYHMNSLDTZ
YMJHFUYNTSGJSJFYMNYWFS
```

You have no idea what it is about, so how would you go
about breaking the encryption? If you know that it has been
encrypted with the Caesar cipher, then one way to break it
is to try all possible shifts and see if you get a meaningful
plaintext from the ciphertext. Essentially, this means running the decryption algorithm for different values of n. You
start with $n = 1$; if the ciphertext does not decrypt to something that makes sense, you go on with $n = 2$; if you fail again
to decrypt, you try $n = 3$; and in the worst case, you will need

to check 26 different values for n. This is again a brute-force method, as you just try out all possible solutions.

Frequency Analysis

There is, however, a better method, and it is here that we go back to the letter frequency counts at the start of the chapter. We use them to perform *frequency analysis*, a staple of *cryptanalysis*, the process of breaking ciphers. If you take a good look at the message, you will see that not all letters appear as often; some letters seem to appear many more times than the rest. For example, if you take the trouble to count exactly how many times each letter appears, you will find out that E appears only once, while J is the most frequent letter, appearing 91 times in total. This should give you an idea: If J is the most frequent letter, then perhaps it has been substituted for E. Similarly, if E is the least frequent character, then perhaps it has been substituted for Z, which is the least frequent character in English. Both substitutions correspond to a shift of 5 places in the alphabet. So you can try decrypting the message as if it were encrypted with the Caesar cipher and a key equal to 5. Here is what you will get:

THEHALLWAYSMELTOFBOILEDCABBAGEANDOL
DRAGMATSATONEENDOFITACOLOUREDPOSTER

```
TOOLARGEFORINDOORDISPLAYHADBEENTACKE
DTOTHEWALLITDEPICTEDSIMPLYANENORMOUS
FACEMORETHANAMETREWIDETHEFACEOFAMA
NOFABOUTFORTYFIVEWITHAHEAVYBLACKMOU
STACHEANDRUGGEDLYHANDSOMEFEATURESWI
NSTONMADEFORTHESTAIRSITWASNOUSETRYIN
GTHELIFTEVENATTHEBESTOFTIMESITWASSELD
OMWORKINGANDATPRESENTTHEELECTRICCUR
RENTWASCUTOFFDURINGDAYLIGHTHOURSITW
ASPARTOFTHEECONOMYDRIVEINPREPARATION
FORHATEWEEKTHEFLATWASSEVENFLIGHTSUPA
NDWINSTONWHOWASTHIRTYNINEANDHADAVA
RICOSEULCERABOVEHISRIGHTANKLEWENTSLO
WLYRESTINGSEVERALTIMESONTHEWAYONEAC
HLANDINGOPPOSITETHELIFTSHAFTTHEPOSTE
RWITHTHEENORMOUSFACEGAZEDFROMTHEW
ALLITWASONEOFTHOSEPICTURESWHICHARESO
CONTRIVEDTHATTHEEYESFOLLOWYOUABOUT
WHENYOUMOVEBIGBROTHERISWATCHINGYOU
THECAPTIONBENEATHITRAN
```

It is not difficult to pick apart the different words; this is
an excerpt from the opening of George Orwell's book *1984*.
This breaking of the encryption is ridiculously easy, and a
computer can do the letter counting in just a few lines of
code. The Caesar cipher is a weak cipher because it pulls
only a threadbare piece of wool over our eyes. It changes

```
A B C D E F G H I J K L M N O P Q R S T U V W X Y Z
↓ ↓ ↓ ↓ ↓ ↓ ↓ ↓ ↓ ↓ ↓ ↓ ↓ ↓ ↓ ↓ ↓ ↓ ↓ ↓ ↓ ↓ ↓ ↓ ↓ ↓
D C V T S O M P J B U L W G F I R Q E Z Y H A N X K
```

Figure 5

the plaintext, but it keeps all the regularities and patterns in it intact. As long as we take notice of this, any notion of secrecy conferred by the cipher is immediately broken.

You may complain that we cheated because this is a message with no punctuation and all letters have been converted to uppercase. Adding punctuation and case would not make much difference: the frequencies of punctuation marks have also been counted in English, and we know that the space is a bit more frequent than E, so it would be easy to spot word boundaries. In fact, if we find word boundaries, decryption is often easier because you can guess individual words. Also, in most texts, the vast majority of letters are lowercase, so the mixture of some uppercase would not pose too much of a difficulty for the analysis.

The Caesar cipher is probably the most straightforward substitution cipher; in general, it is not necessary that we substitute with a shift. We could also just shuffle the letters of the alphabet and decide to substitute, say, D for A, C for B, and so on. The key that we use for encryption and decryption is then a mapping table, shown in figure 5.

To decrypt, we use exactly the same mapping, only reversed, as in figure 6.

Figure 6

The history of cryptography is really one of creative destruction: cipher methods are invented, then they are broken, then better ones are invented, waiting to be broken, or rather hoping that they won't. In this spirit, the substitution cipher that uses a mapping table is an improvement over the Caesar cipher, where the key is just a number that we can find by identifying the most common symbol in the ciphertext, or by brute force.

Indeed, in this cipher, brute force is no longer an effective option to find the cipher key. There are 26 different letters that we can map to A. After we choose one of them for the mapping, there remain 25 different letters that we can map to B. After that, there remain 24 letters that we can map to C. Going on like that, we see that there are $26 \times 25 \times \cdots \times 1 = 26!$ different mapping tables. If you have not come across the notation, $n!$ is the product of all integers from 1 up to and including n: $n! = n \times (n-1) \times (n-2) \times 1$, while by convention $0! = 1$. The number $n!$ is called the *factorial* of n. We come across factorials often in cryptography, as $n!$ gives us all the possible combinations of n elements. Factorials grow very quickly. To realize how big factorials can get, $26! = 4.03291461126605635584 \times 10^{26}$. That is a

The history of cryptography is really one of creative destruction: cipher methods are invented, then they are broken, then better ones are invented, waiting to be broken, or rather hoping that they won't.

number with 27 decimal digits. Trying all possible mapping tables until we find the right one does not seem like a good idea.

Brute force may not be a good option, but frequency analysis is still a formidable ally. If the substitution cipher uses a mapping table, then the most common symbol will give us the way to decrypt only one letter, the most common one. But there is no reason to stop there; we can find the second most common symbol in the ciphertext, which probably corresponds to the second most common letter in English, and so on for the third, fourth, and less frequent letters. Moreover, it is not just individual letters that appear with specific frequencies; we find regularities in combinations of letters as well. Sequences of two letters are called *bigrams*, and sequences of any number of letters are called *n-grams*. We have frequency counts for bigrams and n-grams up to a few characters long. For example, *TH* is the most common bigram in English, so if we find the two most common adjacent symbols in the ciphertext, there is a good chance that they stand for *TH*.

True, it is possible that in a given plaintext, letters and bigrams might not follow exactly the frequencies that prevail in English, or the ciphertext may be too short for the frequencies to emerge. But in general, it is unlikely that they differ a lot. If the most common letter is not *E*, it might be *T*; you can bet that it is not *Q*. You may need to do some guesswork to find all the letter mappings, but note that as you find some of them, you can substitute the mapped letters in the ciphertext so that the plaintext will start making sense and you can make out parts of words. The more characters you decrypt, the easier it gets, much like a jigsaw puzzle.

The efficacy of frequency analysis for code breaking has been known for a long time; the oldest extant source comes from ninth-century Arab scholar and scientist Abū Yūsuf Ya'qūb ibn 'Ishāq aṣ-Ṣabbāḥ al-Kindī (801–873), known as al-Kindī, or under the Latinized Alkindus. Al-Kindī was born in Basra, educated in Baghdad, and active in the House of Wisdom, a major intellectual institution in that city. He contributed to many fields, writing hundreds of treatises. One of the books he wrote is *Risāla fī Istikhrāj al-Kutub al-Mu'amāh* (*On Extracting Obscured Correspondence*, or *On Decrypting Encrypted Correspondence*), where we find the following description of frequency analysis:

> One way to solve an encrypted message, if we know its [original] language, is to find a [different clear] text of the same language long enough to fill one sheet or so, and then we count [the occurrences] of each letter. We call the most frequently occurring letter the "first," the next most occurring letter the "second," the following most occurring letter the "third," and so on, until we account for all the different letters in the cleartext sample. Then we

look at the cipher text we want to solve and we also classify its symbols. We find the most occurring symbol and change it to the form of the "first" letter [of the cleartext sample], the next most common symbol is changed to the form of the "second" letter, and the following most common symbol is changed to the form of the "third" letter, and so on, until we account for all symbols of the cryptogram we want to solve.[9]

The Arab world contributed to cryptography in another, perhaps less obvious way. The word "cipher" comes from the Arabic *sifr*. The original meaning was "empty," but when the Arabs adopted the Indian numerals, which included zero, they translated the Sanskrit word for zero, *sunya*, meaning empty, to the Arab equivalent. Once sifr became zero, its corrupted form "cipher" came to mean "number" in European languages (e.g., *chiffre* in French). The word cipher also came to be used sometimes in the sense of "computation." Yet the concept of zero was initially so baffling that cipher was also used to denote something obscure and incomprehensible, making the link to cryptography.[10]

Stronger Ciphers

The problem with substitution ciphers remains that we only substitute an alphabet for another one. Therefore everything that is written in the plaintext is transferred in exactly the same way in the new alphabet—the ciphertext *looks* different, but it is only a fixed transliteration. Such ciphers are called *monoalphabetic ciphers*, and frequency analysis will promptly break them.

The next step in building more secure cryptographic systems is to consider *polyalphabetic ciphers*, where we do not use a fixed substitution rule—that is, we do not use the same mapping throughout the plaintext. For example, at some point in the plaintext we would substitute X for A to get the ciphertext, at some other point D for A, and we would continue like this, changing the mapping of A to different characters.

We can create a polyalphabetic cipher by putting two alphabets on a disk so that one of them can be rotated in relation to the other, creating a *cipher disk* or *cipher wheel*, portrayed in figure 7.

The outer alphabet is stationary, but the inner alphabet is put on a rotating plate. The cipher works by substituting letters from one alphabet to the matching letter from the other alphabet. As we rotate the plate of the inner alphabet, the mapping changes. The first cipher disk from the left maps A to F; the second one, to Q; and the third one, to H. If the rotating plate contains a scrambled alphabet, as above, then for each position of the rotating plate we get a different mapping-based substitution cipher. If the rotating plate contains a sorted alphabet, we get a different Caesar cipher.

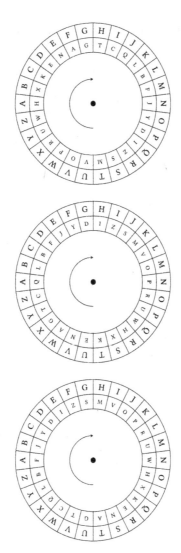

Figure 7

Cryptographers like to use fictional characters to illustrate their methods. When two persons take part in an interchange, they are usually called Alice and Bob. If there is a third participant, they are called Carol, Carlos, or Charlie. Particular letters are reserved for specific roles. Eve is an *eavesdropper* who listens to the conversation between Alice and Bob and tries to understand what they say.

Now if Alice and Bob want to communicate with a cipher disk, they must agree on the disk settings they are going to use. They can do that by agreeing on a string of characters, such as FQHONRUTDJ. This will be their key. Then Alice takes her plaintext and rotates the plate of the cipher disk so that F is below A. She encrypts the first letter of the plaintext using the resulting mapping. If the plaintext goes MEETYOUTOMORROW, M will be mapped to U, so the first letter of the ciphertext will be U. Then she rotates the disk so that Q is below A. The second letter of the plaintext, E, will then be mapped to J. Alice will rotate the plate so that the third letter of the key, H, falls under A; then the third letter of the ciphertext, E, will become N. Note that the letter E was mapped in two different ways in the ciphertext. Alice will continue the encryption in this manner. When she reaches the tenth character of the plaintext, M from TOMORROW, she will exhaust the key. As the message has more than ten characters, she will continue encrypting by starting from the beginning of the key again. She will rotate the disk to place F under A, and

O will be mapped to *H*. Then she will continue to the end of the plaintext, reusing the key as many times as required (in this example, the key is reused only once). To decrypt the message, Bob will work in the same way, but mapping from the inner to the outer alphabet, rotating the plate according to the key.

The crucial feature of this cipher is that, as we saw, the same letter can be encrypted differently in the ciphertext. If we count the frequencies of the letters, we will not find a correspondence with the frequencies that we would expect. Even if in the plaintext the letter *E* is the most common symbol, in the ciphertext this will no longer hold. It is not possible to break a polyalphabetic cipher with frequency analysis as we have described it. For this reason, these ciphers gained a notoriety for being unbreakable and, indeed, it took quite some time to find a way around the problem.

Polyalphabetic ciphers were developed in the European Renaissance. The first-known cipher to work along these lines was proposed by Florentine Leon Battista Alberti around 1467. Alberti was the quintessential renaissance man, surpassed perhaps only by Leonardo da Vinci in his accomplishments. In cryptography, apart from inventing the cipher disk, he was the author of the earliest extant cryptanalysis text in the West, in which he described frequency analysis.[11] The idea of polyalphabetic substitution was taken further by Johannes Trithemius, a monk in the Holy

Roman Empire who dabbled in theology, occult writings, and, perhaps unavoidably, the art of hiding secrets. Trithemius's *Polygraphia* is the first published book on the subject, printed in July 1518. The ciphers were taken another step forward by an ecclesiastical courtier, Giovan Battista Bellaso, about whom almost nothing is known except for a booklet on encrypting messages, *La cifra del. Sig. Giovan Battista Bellaso (The Cipher of Mr. Giovan Battista Bellaso)*, published in 1553. After Bellaso, a young Neapolitan, Giovanni Battista Porta, published at the age of twenty-six *De Furtivis Literarum Notis (On Concealed Characters in Writing)*, an extraordinary book on ciphers and cryptography in which he further advanced polyalphabetic ciphers. Gerolamo Cardano (1501–1576), a Pavoan polymath and mathematician, also worked on ciphers, although he did not achieve much. Cardano longed to be remembered in the generations to come; indeed, today he is remembered not for his work on cryptography, where he ended up a bit player, but instead as one of the founders of probability theory and for his contributions to the development of algebra.

In one of history's ironic twists, the person most associated with polyalphabetic ciphers was none of the above, but rather a Frenchman, Blaise de Vigenère (1523–1596). A polyalphabetic cipher called the Vigenère cipher was long thought to be impervious to any attacks—although the so-called Vigenère cipher had nothing to do with Vigenère himself, who would probably not deign to be associated with it, as the Vigenère cipher is really a weakened version of the ciphers the man produced.

The Vigenère cipher is a tabular version of the cipher disk. Rotated alphabets are placed in rows, forming a square; we add two alphabets, as seen in figure 8 on the top and left for convenience, to act as indexes.

If we want to encrypt ATTACKATDAWN, we select a key, which we repeat as many times as needed to cover the plaintext, as we would do with a cipher disk. Suppose that we start with LEMON; our key will be LEMONLEMONLE. We take the first letter of the plaintext and find it in the alphabet at the top. We then take the first letter of the key and find it in the alphabet on the left. We find the intersection of the plaintext letter column and key letter row; this will be the encrypted letter—L, in our case. It does not matter that it happens to be the same with the plaintext letter—in fact, we'll see later that this is a good thing. We repeat the same process for all the remaining letters of the plaintext. For the second letter, shown in figure 8 on page 31, the result of the encryption is at the intersection of column T and row E, so it will be X. If we continue in this way, the plaintext will be encrypted to LXFOPVEFRNHR.

Decryption using the Vigenère cipher is similar. If we have the ciphertext LXFOPVEFRNHR, we go to the Vigenère square and take the first letter of the key and first letter of the ciphertext, as you can see in figure 9 on page 32.

	A	B	C	D	E	F	G	H	I	J	K	L	M	N	O	P	Q	R	S	T	U	V	W	X	Y	Z
A	A	B	C	D	E	F	G	H	I	J	K	L	M	N	O	P	Q	R	S	T	U	V	W	X	Y	Z
B	B	C	D	E	F	G	H	I	J	K	L	M	N	O	P	Q	R	S	T	U	V	W	X	Y	Z	A
C	C	D	E	F	G	H	I	J	K	L	M	N	O	P	Q	R	S	T	U	V	W	X	Y	Z	A	B
D	D	E	F	G	H	I	J	K	L	M	N	O	P	Q	R	S	T	U	V	W	X	Y	Z	A	B	C
E	E	F	G	H	I	J	K	L	M	N	O	P	Q	R	S	T	U	V	W	X	Y	Z	A	B	C	D
F	F	G	H	I	J	K	L	M	N	O	P	Q	R	S	T	U	V	W	X	Y	Z	A	B	C	D	E
G	G	H	I	J	K	L	M	N	O	P	Q	R	S	T	U	V	W	X	Y	Z	A	B	C	D	E	F
H	H	I	J	K	L	M	N	O	P	Q	R	S	T	U	V	W	X	Y	Z	A	B	C	D	E	F	G
I	I	J	K	L	M	N	O	P	Q	R	S	T	U	V	W	X	Y	Z	A	B	C	D	E	F	H	H
J	J	K	L	M	N	O	P	Q	R	S	T	U	V	W	X	Y	Z	A	B	C	D	E	F	H	I	I
K	K	L	M	N	O	P	Q	R	S	T	U	V	W	X	Y	Z	A	B	C	D	E	F	H	I	J	J
L	L	M	N	O	P	Q	R	S	T	U	V	W	X	Y	Z	A	B	C	D	E	F	H	I	J	J	K
M	M	N	O	P	Q	R	S	T	U	V	W	X	Y	Z	A	B	C	D	E	F	H	I	J	J	K	L
N	N	O	P	Q	R	S	T	U	V	W	X	Y	Z	A	B	C	D	E	F	H	I	J	J	K	L	M
O	O	P	Q	R	S	T	U	V	W	X	Y	Z	A	B	C	D	E	F	G	H	I	J	K	L	M	N
P	P	Q	R	S	T	U	V	W	X	Y	Z	A	B	C	D	E	F	G	H	I	J	K	L	M	N	O
Q	Q	R	S	T	U	V	W	X	Y	Z	A	B	C	D	E	F	G	H	I	J	K	L	M	N	O	P
R	R	S	T	U	V	W	X	Y	Z	A	B	C	D	E	F	G	H	I	J	K	L	M	N	O	P	Q
S	S	T	U	V	W	X	Y	Z	A	B	C	D	E	F	G	H	I	J	K	L	M	N	O	P	Q	R
T	T	U	V	W	X	Y	Z	A	B	C	D	E	F	H	I	J	J	K	L	M	N	O	P	Q	R	S
U	U	V	W	X	Y	Z	A	B	C	D	E	F	G	H	I	J	K	L	M	N	O	P	Q	R	S	T
V	V	W	X	Y	Z	A	B	C	D	E	F	G	H	I	J	K	L	M	N	O	P	Q	R	S	T	U
W	W	X	Y	Z	A	B	C	D	E	F	G	H	I	J	K	L	M	N	O	P	Q	R	S	T	U	V
X	X	Y	Z	A	B	C	D	E	F	G	H	I	J	K	L	M	N	O	P	Q	R	S	T	U	V	W
Y	Y	Z	A	B	C	D	E	F	G	H	I	J	K	L	M	N	O	P	Q	R	S	T	U	V	W	X
Z	Z	A	B	C	D	E	F	G	H	I	J	K	L	M	N	O	P	Q	R	S	T	U	V	W	X	Y

Figure 8

	A	B	C	D	E	F	G	H	I	J	K	L	M	N	O	P	Q	R	S	T	U	V	W	X	Y	Z
A	A	B	C	D	E	F	G	H	I	J	K	L	M	N	O	P	Q	R	S	T	U	V	W	X	Y	Z
B	B	C	D	E	F	G	H	I	J	K	L	M	N	O	P	Q	R	S	T	U	V	W	X	Y	Z	A
C	C	D	E	F	G	H	I	J	K	L	M	N	O	P	Q	R	S	T	U	V	W	X	Y	Z	A	B
D	D	E	F	G	H	I	J	K	L	M	N	O	P	Q	R	S	T	U	V	W	X	Y	Z	A	B	C
E	E	F	G	H	I	J	K	L	M	N	O	P	Q	R	S	T	U	V	W	X	Y	Z	A	B	C	D
F	F	G	H	I	J	K	L	M	N	O	P	Q	R	S	T	U	V	W	X	Y	Z	A	B	C	D	E
G	G	H	I	J	K	L	M	N	O	P	Q	R	S	T	U	V	W	X	Y	Z	A	B	C	D	E	F
H	H	I	J	K	L	M	N	O	P	Q	R	S	T	U	V	W	X	Y	Z	A	B	C	D	E	F	G
I	I	J	K	L	M	N	O	P	Q	R	S	T	U	V	W	X	Y	Z	A	B	C	D	E	F	H	H
J	J	K	L	M	N	O	P	Q	R	S	T	U	V	W	X	Y	Z	A	B	C	D	E	F	H	I	I
K	K	L	M	N	O	P	Q	R	S	T	U	V	W	X	Y	Z	A	B	C	D	E	F	H	I	J	J
L	L	M	N	O	P	Q	R	S	T	U	V	W	X	Y	Z	A	B	C	D	E	F	H	I	J	J	K
M	M	N	O	P	Q	R	S	T	U	V	W	X	Y	Z	A	B	C	D	E	F	H	I	J	J	K	L
N	N	O	P	Q	R	S	T	U	V	W	X	Y	Z	A	B	C	D	E	F	H	I	J	J	K	L	M
O	O	P	Q	R	S	T	U	V	W	X	Y	Z	A	B	C	D	E	F	G	H	I	J	K	L	M	N
P	P	Q	R	S	T	U	V	W	X	Y	Z	A	B	C	D	E	F	G	H	I	J	K	L	M	N	O
Q	Q	R	S	T	U	V	W	X	Y	Z	A	B	C	D	E	F	G	H	I	J	K	L	M	N	O	P
R	R	S	T	U	V	W	X	Y	Z	A	B	C	D	E	F	G	H	I	J	K	L	M	N	O	P	Q
S	S	T	U	V	W	X	Y	Z	A	B	C	D	E	F	G	H	I	J	K	L	M	N	O	P	Q	R
T	T	U	V	W	X	Y	Z	A	B	C	D	E	F	H	I	J	J	K	L	M	N	O	P	Q	R	S
U	U	V	W	X	Y	Z	A	B	C	D	E	F	G	H	I	J	K	L	M	N	O	P	Q	R	S	T
V	V	W	X	Y	Z	A	B	C	D	E	F	G	H	I	J	K	L	M	N	O	P	Q	R	S	T	U
W	W	X	Y	Z	A	B	C	D	E	F	G	H	I	J	K	L	M	N	O	P	Q	R	S	T	U	V
X	X	Y	Z	A	B	C	D	E	F	G	H	I	J	K	L	M	N	O	P	Q	R	S	T	U	V	W
Y	Y	Z	A	B	C	D	E	F	G	H	I	J	K	L	M	N	O	P	Q	R	S	T	U	V	W	X
Z	Z	A	B	C	D	E	F	G	H	I	J	K	L	M	N	O	P	Q	R	S	T	U	V	W	X	Y

	A	B	C	D	E	F	G	H	I	J	K	L	M	N	O	P	Q	R	S	T	U	V	W	X	Y	Z
A	A	B	C	D	E	F	G	H	I	J	K	L	M	N	O	P	Q	R	S	T	U	V	W	X	Y	Z
B	B	C	D	E	F	G	H	I	J	K	L	M	N	O	P	Q	R	S	T	U	V	W	X	Y	Z	A
C	C	D	E	F	G	H	I	J	K	L	M	N	O	P	Q	R	S	T	U	V	W	X	Y	Z	A	B
D	D	E	F	G	H	I	J	K	L	M	N	O	P	Q	R	S	T	U	V	W	X	Y	Z	A	B	C
E	E	F	G	H	I	J	K	L	M	N	O	P	Q	R	S	T	U	V	W	X	Y	Z	A	B	C	D
F	F	G	H	I	J	K	L	M	N	O	P	Q	R	S	T	U	V	W	X	Y	Z	A	B	C	D	E
G	G	H	I	J	K	L	M	N	O	P	Q	R	S	T	U	V	W	X	Y	Z	A	B	C	D	E	F
H	H	I	J	K	L	M	N	O	P	Q	R	S	T	U	V	W	X	Y	Z	A	B	C	D	E	F	G
I	I	J	K	L	M	N	O	P	Q	R	S	T	U	V	W	X	Y	Z	A	B	C	D	E	F	H	H
J	J	K	L	M	N	O	P	Q	R	S	T	U	V	W	X	Y	Z	A	B	C	D	E	F	H	I	I
K	K	L	M	N	O	P	Q	R	S	T	U	V	W	X	Y	Z	A	B	C	D	E	F	H	I	J	J
L	L	M	N	O	P	Q	R	S	T	U	V	W	X	Y	Z	A	B	C	D	E	F	H	I	J	J	K
M	M	N	O	P	Q	R	S	T	U	V	W	X	Y	Z	A	B	C	D	E	F	H	I	J	J	K	L
N	N	O	P	Q	R	S	T	U	V	W	X	Y	Z	A	B	C	D	E	F	H	I	J	J	K	L	M
O	O	P	Q	R	S	T	U	V	W	X	Y	Z	A	B	C	D	E	F	G	H	I	J	K	L	M	N
P	P	Q	R	S	T	U	V	W	X	Y	Z	A	B	C	D	E	F	G	H	I	J	K	L	M	N	O
Q	Q	R	S	T	U	V	W	X	Y	Z	A	B	C	D	E	F	G	H	I	J	K	L	M	N	O	P
R	R	S	T	U	V	W	X	Y	Z	A	B	C	D	E	F	G	H	I	J	K	L	M	N	O	P	Q
S	S	T	U	V	W	X	Y	Z	A	B	C	D	E	F	G	H	I	J	K	L	M	N	O	P	Q	R
T	T	U	V	W	X	Y	Z	A	B	C	D	E	F	H	I	J	J	K	L	M	N	O	P	Q	R	S
U	U	V	W	X	Y	Z	A	B	C	D	E	F	G	H	I	J	K	L	M	N	O	P	Q	R	S	T
V	V	W	X	Y	Z	A	B	C	D	E	F	G	H	I	J	K	L	M	N	O	P	Q	R	S	T	U
W	W	X	Y	Z	A	B	C	D	E	F	G	H	I	J	K	L	M	N	O	P	Q	R	S	T	U	V
X	X	Y	Z	A	B	C	D	E	F	G	H	I	J	K	L	M	N	O	P	Q	R	S	T	U	V	W
Y	Y	Z	A	B	C	D	E	F	G	H	I	J	K	L	M	N	O	P	Q	R	S	T	U	V	W	X
Z	Z	A	B	C	D	E	F	G	H	I	J	K	L	M	N	O	P	Q	R	S	T	U	V	W	X	Y

Figure 9

	A	B	C	D	E	F	G	H	I	J	K	L	M	N	O	P	Q	R	S	T	U	V	W	X	Y	Z
A	A	B	C	D	E	F	G	H	I	J	K	L	M	N	O	P	Q	R	S	T	U	V	W	X	Y	Z
B	B	C	D	E	F	G	H	I	J	K	L	M	N	O	P	Q	R	S	T	U	V	W	X	Y	Z	A
C	C	D	E	F	G	H	I	J	K	L	M	N	O	P	Q	R	S	T	U	V	W	X	Y	Z	A	B
D	D	E	F	G	H	I	J	K	L	M	N	O	P	Q	R	S	T	U	V	W	X	Y	Z	A	B	C
E	E	F	G	H	I	J	K	L	M	N	O	P	Q	R	S	T	U	V	W	X	Y	Z	A	B	C	D
F	F	G	H	I	J	K	L	M	N	O	P	Q	R	S	T	U	V	W	X	Y	Z	A	B	C	D	E
G	G	H	I	J	K	L	M	N	O	P	Q	R	S	T	U	V	W	X	Y	Z	A	B	C	D	E	F
H	H	I	J	K	L	M	N	O	P	Q	R	S	T	U	V	W	X	Y	Z	A	B	C	D	E	F	G
I	I	J	K	L	M	N	O	P	Q	R	S	T	U	V	W	X	Y	Z	A	B	C	D	E	F	H	H
J	J	K	L	M	N	O	P	Q	R	S	T	U	V	W	X	Y	Z	A	B	C	D	E	F	H	I	I
K	K	L	M	N	O	P	Q	R	S	T	U	V	W	X	Y	Z	A	B	C	D	E	F	H	I	J	J
L	L	M	N	O	P	Q	R	S	T	U	V	W	X	Y	Z	A	B	C	D	E	F	H	I	J	J	K
M	M	N	O	P	Q	R	S	T	U	V	W	X	Y	Z	A	B	C	D	E	F	H	I	J	J	K	L
N	N	O	P	Q	R	S	T	U	V	W	X	Y	Z	A	B	C	D	E	F	H	I	J	J	K	L	M
O	O	P	Q	R	S	T	U	V	W	X	Y	Z	A	B	C	D	E	F	G	H	I	J	K	L	M	N
P	P	Q	R	S	T	U	V	W	X	Y	Z	A	B	C	D	E	F	G	H	I	J	K	L	M	N	O
Q	Q	R	S	T	U	V	W	X	Y	Z	A	B	C	D	E	F	G	H	I	J	K	L	M	N	O	P
R	R	S	T	U	V	W	X	Y	Z	A	B	C	D	E	F	G	H	I	J	K	L	M	N	O	P	Q
S	S	T	U	V	W	X	Y	Z	A	B	C	D	E	F	G	H	I	J	K	L	M	N	O	P	Q	R
T	T	U	V	W	X	Y	Z	A	B	C	D	E	F	H	I	J	J	K	L	M	N	O	P	Q	R	S
U	U	V	W	X	Y	Z	A	B	C	D	E	F	G	H	I	J	K	L	M	N	O	P	Q	R	S	T
V	V	W	X	Y	Z	A	B	C	D	E	F	G	H	I	J	K	L	M	N	O	P	Q	R	S	T	U
W	W	X	Y	Z	A	B	C	D	E	F	G	H	I	J	K	L	M	N	O	P	Q	R	S	T	U	V
X	X	Y	Z	A	B	C	D	E	F	G	H	I	J	K	L	M	N	O	P	Q	R	S	T	U	V	W
Y	Y	Z	A	B	C	D	E	F	G	H	I	J	K	L	M	N	O	P	Q	R	S	T	U	V	W	X
Z	Z	A	B	C	D	E	F	G	H	I	J	K	L	M	N	O	P	Q	R	S	T	U	V	W	X	Y

We use the letter of the key as an index to the key column on the left and select the L row. In the selected row, we search for the ciphertext letter, L. Once we find it, we go up the column to get the corresponding letter in the horizontal alphabet on top; this gives us the letter A. We continue with the second key letter, E, and the second ciphertext letter, X. We select the E row, find the X letter in it, and select the corresponding column. This will give us the letter T in the horizontal alphabet at the top of page 33. If we do that for all the remaining letters, we'll get the original plaintext.

Polyalphabetic ciphers were broken in the nineteenth century, first by Charles Babbage (1791–1871), a forebearer of computing who designed mechanical computers that would operate using the technologies known at his time. Although his machines were not in fact built in his lifetime, his *analytical engine* incorporated the main ideas that underlie the digital computers that were eventually built several decades after his death. Having reached Babbage, it would be completely amiss not to mention Ada Lovelace, Lord Byron's daughter and a gifted mathematician. Lovelace corresponded with Babbage and is credited as being the world's first programmer, as she developed an algorithm that would operate on Babbage's analytical engine.

Babbage worked on a variant of the Vigenère cipher and found the way to break it in 1854, but he did not publish his work (throughout his life he seemed to have a problem with finishing things). It was a bit later, in 1863, that a German infantry officer, archaeologist, and cryptographer, Friedrich Kasiski, published the book *Die Geheimschriften und die Dechiffrir-Kunst* (*Secret Writing and the Art of Deciphering*), containing the first detailed attack on polyalphabetic ciphers. In another of history's twisted turns, Kasiski did not realize the importance of his findings and turned to archaeology, joined the Natural Science Society of Danzig (present-day Gdańsk in Poland), excavated prehistoric graves, wrote articles on the subject, and died in 1881 oblivious that his book was a revolution in cryptography.

The weakness of the Vigenère cipher comes from the limitations of the key. It works by choosing a different encrypted character, based on a character of the key. But as we saw, at some point we come to the end of the key, and then we have to wrap around and start reusing the key from the start.

As the Vigenère cipher is essentially a tabular version of the cipher disk, let's see what happens with the disk. If we have a ten-letter key, after ten characters we will rotate the cipher disk back to its initial position, and this will happen every ten characters. That means that if we take every tenth character of our plaintext, these characters will all be encrypted using the *same* alphabet; for all of them, the plate of the cipher disk will be rotated in the same position. The same thing will happen with the second character of the plaintext and every tenth character starting from the second; all of them will be encrypted with the same rotation of the cipher disk. In the end, characters 1, 11, 21, . . . are encrypted with a single mapping, characters 2, 12, 22, . . . are encrypted with a single mapping, up to characters 10, 10, 100, . . . It is as if we had split the plaintext message in ten different parts and used a simple substitution cipher to encrypt each part. If our key were longer than ten characters, exactly the same principle would apply, only we would not take every tenth character, but we would proceed with some longer stride between characters.

Suppose that we want to encrypt a plaintext with a key that is thirteen characters long. The encryption process with the cipher disk is equivalent to reformatting our plaintext so that it flows in rows that are thirteen characters wide and then encrypting each column with a monoalphabetic substitution cipher. The excerpt from 1984 that we saw before would go like what's depicted in figure 10.

The characters line up in columns; the last row is our thirteen-character key. All the first column is encrypted with the cipher disk in the same configuration: I under A; all the second column is encrypted with the cipher disk configured with Q under A; and so on. In the Vigenère cipher the situation is similar: all the first column is encrypted with the same alphabet, indicated by the key letter I in the Vigenère table; all the second column is encrypted

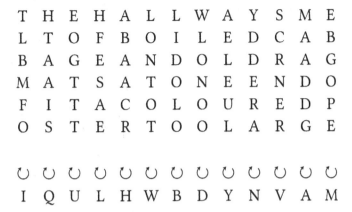

T	H	E	H	A	L	L	W	A	Y	S	M	E
L	T	O	F	B	O	I	L	E	D	C	A	B
B	A	G	E	A	N	D	O	L	D	R	A	G
M	A	T	S	A	T	O	N	E	E	N	D	O
F	I	T	A	C	O	L	O	U	R	E	D	P
O	S	T	E	R	T	O	O	L	A	R	G	E

∪	∪	∪	∪	∪	∪	∪	∪	∪	∪	∪	∪	∪
I	Q	U	L	H	W	B	D	Y	N	V	A	M

Figure 10

with the same alphabet, indicated by the key letter Q in the table; and the last column is encrypted by the alphabet indicated by the key letter M.

Once we know that, we are a short step away from breaking the cipher: we can perform a frequency analysis of the ciphertext *for each column separately*. As the same substitution cipher is used throughout the column, the encrypted letters will display the frequencies that we would expect. Running multiple frequency analyses is certainly more effort than running a single one, but not prohibitively so; the only thing that we need for our strategy to work is the length of the key so that we can arrange the characters of the ciphertext in the correct number of columns.

```
C A K E C A K E C A K E C A K E C A K E C A K E C A K E
S E C U R E T H E K E Y T O E N S U R E S E C U R I T Y
U E M Y T E D L G K O C V O O R U U B I U E M Y T I D C
```

Figure 11

To find the length of the key, we may exploit the fact that the same part of the plaintext can end up encrypted in the same way in the ciphertext. For example, suppose that the plaintext is SECURETHEKEYTOENSURESECU-RITY, and the key is CAKE. If we go back to the Vigenère cipher to encrypt the message, we'll get UEMYTEDLG-KOCVOORUUBIUEMYTIDC, as seen in figure 11.

If we are the adversary and have intercepted the ciphertext, we can spot that UEMYT appears twice in it. It is likely then that this is the result of the same part of the plaintext being encrypted in the same way. The two occurrences of UEMYT appear twenty characters apart. The identical encryption can happen if the key is twenty characters long or some number that divides twenty—that is, the factors of twenty: one, two, four, five, or ten. We can discount one and two because they are too short. We can then try frequency analysis by arranging the text in four, five, or ten columns, and see which arrangement decrypts the message.

That is a fundamental weakness for polyalphabetic ciphers: if the key is repeated, they are really repeated applications of polyalphabetic ciphers, and these are easy to break. Which suggests, Would it be possible for the key not to be repeated?

The Perfect Cipher

The problem that arises with key repetition in polyalphabetic ciphers suggests a radical solution: do away with repetition altogether. This leads not just to a more secure cipher but also to the only cipher that is truly unbreakable and will remain so forever. Yes, such a thing exists, and we have known about it since shortly after polyalphabetic ciphers were broken. It was first described in 1882 by Frank Miller (1842–1925). Miller was a Sacramento banker and trustee of Stanford University who was interested in cryptography too. The unbreakable cipher was then reinvented in 1917 by Gilbert Vernam, an engineer at AT&T Bell Labs, and Joseph Mauborgne, a captain in the US Army and later chief of the Signal Corps.[12]

The unbreakable cipher rests on two premises: first, we have a key that is as long as our message. Second, the key is completely random. The first premise ensures that the key won't be repeated during encryption. The second premise ensures that the ciphertext will also be random and all regularities that would help us break the encryption will be completely eliminated.

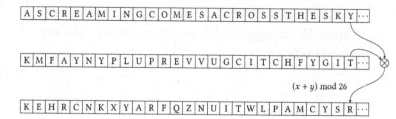

Figure 12

Once we have a plaintext message and completely random key that covers the whole message, we work as follows. We put the message and key so that one character of the message corresponds to one character of the key. For example, in figure 12, we can align them one under the other.

The result of encryption comes from taking the two characters from the plaintext and key, treating them as numbers (*A* is 0, *B* is 1, . . .), and adding them together. If the result takes us beyond the end of the alphabet (a value greater than or equal to 26), then we wrap around the start of the alphabet. This, as we saw, is what we do with the modulo operation. The encryption algorithm is:

1. Take the next letter of the plaintext. If there is no letter, stop.

2. Take the next letter of the key.

3. Get the numerical value, say x, corresponding to the plaintext letter, and the numerical value, say y, corresponding to the key letter.

4. Output the value $(x + y)$ mod 26.

The same character can be mapped to any character of the alphabet in the ciphertext, as it may be combined with any random character. It may even happen that a character is mapped to itself, as happens in the fourth character, R, of the plaintext in our example. As we have remarked, this is actually a good thing. If we know that a character *cannot* be mapped to itself, that is a major weakness in a cryptographic system because this information can help decryption efforts by ruling out possible mappings. Crucially, the complete randomness of the output means that, as the key is not repeated, there is no subset of the ciphertext letters to which we may apply frequency analysis.

Decryption is almost the same as encryption. We take each character of the ciphertext and key, only this time we subtract the corresponding values, as portrayed in figure 13:

1. Take the next letter of the ciphertext. If there is no letter, stop.

2. Take the next letter of the key.

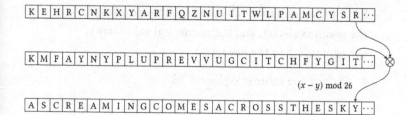

Figure 13

3. Get the numerical value, say x, corresponding to the ciphertext letter, and the numerical value, say y, corresponding to the key letter.

4. Output the value $(x - y) \bmod 26$.

As we go through the encryption and decryption, we use each letter of the key only once. It is as if we were using a pad and striking out letters from it; indeed, the method is called *one-time pad*.

The one-time pad can never be broken because we have nothing to hold onto to base our decryption efforts. By taking the ciphertext and mixing it with something completely random, we obtain something completely random. No matter how carefully we may examine the ciphertext, we'll find no clues to the key. We may try to guess the key with a brute-force method. If the message and key are long enough, that is going to be impractical. To find the first character of the key, we may have to try each of the 26 letters of the alphabet. Then we have to do the same for the second character of the key. That means 26×26 possibilities for the first two characters of the key. Similarly, any of the 26 characters of the alphabet may come third in the key, meaning $26 \times 26 \times 26$ possibilities for the first three characters. And so on and so forth, up to the last character of the key. If the key is n characters long, we may have to check $\overbrace{26 \times 26 \times \cdots \times 26}^{n} = 26^n$ different keys. This number is huge for anything but short messages. A line of text in a printed book may be around 70 characters. If our message is a single line with 70 characters, the key would also be 70 characters long, and it would be one out of 26^{70} possible keys. A slightly longer message of 100 characters would have 26^{100} possible keys. That number, written out in full, has 142 digits. Trying 1 million keys per second would require more than a googol of years, where one googol is equal to 10^{100} (yes, you may be familiar with a service named after the number). According to the current estimates, our universe is approximately about 13.77 billion years old, which is 13.77×10^9. The time required to try all keys for such a short message would vastly exceed the time elapsed since the big bang.

Moreover, there is a more insidious problem lurking. Say that as we are trying different keys, we stumble on something that decrypts the ciphertext to a message that makes sense. How can we know it decrypts *to the original message*? For example, take the ciphertext we produced

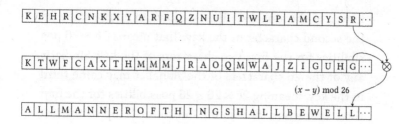

| K | E | H | R | C | N | K | X | Y | A | R | F | Q | Z | N | U | I | T | W | L | P | A | M | C | Y | S | R | ··· |

| K | T | W | F | C | A | X | T | H | M | M | M | J | R | A | O | Q | M | W | A | J | Z | I | G | U | H | G | ··· |

$(x - y) \bmod 26$

| A | L | L | M | A | N | N | E | R | O | F | T | H | I | N | G | S | H | A | L | L | B | E | W | E | L | L | ··· |

Figure 14

above. In our effort to find a key, we may strike on KT WFCAXTHMMMJRAOQMWAJZIGUHG, which decrypts the ciphertext to something perfectly meaningful, shown in figure 14.

The problem is, instead of getting the opening line of Thomas Pynchon's *Gravity's Rainbow*, we got one of the closing lines of T. S. Elliot's *Little Gidding*.

This can always happen. The message ATTACKATD AWN encrypted with the key LJBLUKLPIBEW becomes LCULWULILBAJ. If we use the key LJBLUKLPYNMW, however, it decrypts beautifully to ATTACKATNOON, and who's to tell us that this is the wrong key and not the correct decryption? It is not the enormous size of the different keys that we may have to try in order to break the one-time pad but instead the fact that any decryption is possible. A brute-force attack is a fool's errand.

We have found a perfect encryption scheme, which brings up the question, Why is the issue not closed? It would seem that cryptography should have ended with the invention of the one-time pad, but it did not.

The reason cryptography has continued evolving has to do with the two premises on which the one-time pad is based. Remember, the key must be completely random and cover the whole plaintext so that it is never repeated. Both assumptions make the one-time pad difficult to use in practice.

First, take the randomness of the key. It is not easy at all to generate a large sequence of random symbols. You can use unloaded dice and coins, or a roulette wheel, but that does not scale up well. A message might have thousands and thousands of characters, so you would need thousands and thousands of throws.

A possibility would be to use a computer to generate random numbers, but that is not easy either. A computer can only follow a prescribed sequence of steps. Since the steps are known in advance, the computer works along the path we have planned for it; that is not random. An algorithm is a deterministic way to do things: How can you generate something unpredictable through a completely predetermined course of events? As computer pioneer John von Neumann remarked, "Any one who considers arithmetical methods of producing random digits is, of course, in a state of sin."[13] The best way to generate random numbers is to have access to a physical source of randomness, like radioactive decay or thermal noise.

Such methods are cumbersome and expensive. You can use random events inside a computer. Modern computer processors contain integrated components that provide true random numbers based on nondeterministic hardware processes. When we need random numbers and do not have recourse to such hardware that can give us the randomness we need, or we need more numbers than it can provide, we use algorithms that produce numbers that look random, although they are not (so we are sinning, but we try to hide it). These are called *pseudorandom*, and the algorithms that produce them are called *pseudorandom number generators*.

As the key must never be repeated in the one-time pad, you must be able to produce random numbers continuously, as long as you have messages to encrypt. Each time the key will be as long as the message, which brings forward another problem: how to distribute the key so that the recipient of the encrypted message can decrypt it. Clearly, you cannot send it along with the message; any interloper would just intercept it and decrypt the message. You must send it through a completely secure channel, which you trust cannot be broken. Otherwise Eve, the eavesdropper, will get the key and then just go along with the decryption. Such secure channels are difficult to establish. A good old-fashioned way is to transfer the key physically and trust the messenger carrying the key. That involves actual travel, so you can imagine that it is not something that can be used easily en masse. The problem is exacerbated if you need to send the message to more than one recipient. Then we need to transfer the key securely to each one of them. The *key distribution problem* is not specific to the one-time pad; you must distribute the key for any polyalphabetic substitution cipher that you want to use. The problem is that it is easier to transfer securely a short key than a long one, particularly a key that has to be as long as the message.

For those reasons, the one-time pad has remained a niche cryptographic method. Some well-organized government agencies or the military may have the resources to apply it to specific uses. It is an elegant proposition, mathematically perfect, but it has not invalidated, nor do we expect it to invalidate, the search for good practical encryption and decryption that can scale to big messages and large volumes of data, and thus can be used by anybody.

Enigma

Before we turn to modern encryption methods, it would be a pity not to mention probably the most famous of encryption devices, the Enigma machine that was used by the Germans in World War II. The breaking of Enigma has been the subject of books and even the popular 2014 feature film *The Imitation Game*. It is not possible to provide a full account here, but it is possible to give an idea of how Enigma worked and some hints as to how it was finally broken.

Enigma is essentially a souped-up substitution cipher. It was implemented as a physical device in a case so that it could be easily carried around, as shown in figure 15.[14]

It involved some clever machinery, which nonetheless can be represented in a single diagram in figure 16.[15]

The heart of Enigma was three cipher disks, called *rotors* (in fact, they were cylinders). A letter that was to be encrypted would be encrypted by the first rotor, then its result would be encrypted by the second rotor, and that result would be encrypted by the third rotor.

Once a letter was encrypted, the first rotor would be rotated one position so that the mapping alphabet would change for the next character. There are 26 characters on the rotor. After 26 shifts of the first rotor, the second rotor would also perform a shift of one position, so every full rotation of the first rotor we would have a shift of one position of the second rotor. It's like the hands of the clock: after a full revolution of the hand showing the seconds along the clockface, the minute hand moves one minute. After a full revolution of the minute hand, the hour hand moves one hour. The same thing happened with the second and third rotor. After a full rotation of the second rotor, the third rotor would shift by one position.

The effect of the three combined cipher disks is that for every setting of the first disk, there are 26 settings of

Figure 15

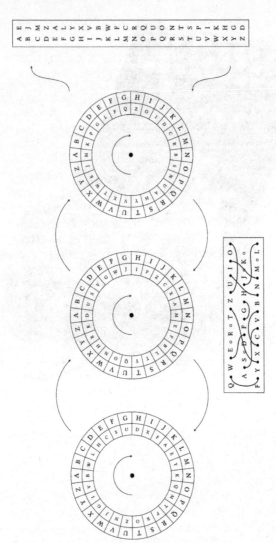

Figure 16

the second disk, and for every setting of the second disk, there are 26 settings of the third disk. In all, there are 26 × 26 × 26 = 17,576 different settings to go through before we return to the initial one.

From figure 16, you can see that there was something underneath the rotors and something to the right of them. The part on the right was called a *reflector*. It functioned as a monoalphabetic substitution cipher, taking the output of the third rotor, making a substitution, and then taking it back to the rotor. Then the encrypted letter would take the reverse route, from the third to the second rotor and then to the first, getting encrypted again along the way. The difference with the way back was that this time the mapping on each disk worked from the inside to the outside. For example, taking the third disk, when going from the left to right, the letter A would be encrypted to M; when going from the right to left, the letter A would be encrypted to R (try to find A in the inner disk). The reflector made the Enigma *self-reciprocal*, meaning that the decryption process was exactly the same as the encryption. It also had an important flaw against which we have cautioned previously: it had the effect that no letter could be mapped to itself. This effect could give hints to cryptanalysts that might help them in their analysis efforts.

Finally, there was a piece underneath the rotors called a *plugboard*. Ten pairs of letters could be connected with cables, as shown in figure 16, so that one letter would substitute the other. That makes for another (partial) substitution cipher. The plugboard was used twice: before and after the rotors. The plaintext letter would go first to the plugboard, then the output of the plugboard would go to the first rotor, then it would travel along the rotors to the reflector, go back to the rotors, enter the plugboard again, and a final encrypted letter would come out.

Let's see that with an example. Suppose we want to encrypt *W*.

1. *W* is mapped to *D* on the plugboard.

2. We take *D* and find its substitution in the first rotor: *D* becomes *H*.

3. We take *H* and find its substitution in the second rotor: *H* becomes *I*.

4. We take *I* and find its substitution in the third rotor: *I* becomes *O*.

5. *O* enters the reflector and becomes *Q*.

6. *Q* goes back to the third rotor and becomes *G*.

7. *G* goes back to the second rotor and becomes *E*.

8. *E* goes back to the first rotor and becomes *L*.

9. *L* goes to the plugboard and becomes *H*; that is the result of the encryption.

This perhaps made your head spin. The strength of Enigma rests on the difficulty of finding its key. The key depends on the exact settings of the plugboard and rotors at the beginning of the message. The operator would set the rotors and plug the cables as specified by the key, and then would start typing the message that would go through the route we described to produce the ciphertext. To decrypt the ciphertext, the recipient should put the machine at exactly the same configuration as at the beginning of encryption and then type the ciphertext. As encryption and decryption in Enigma are completely symmetric, the original plaintext would come out when the Enigma operator typed in the ciphertext.

As the Enigma settings change after each letter, Enigma will not return to its initial configuration before all three rotors have executed a full rotation. This will take 17,576 letters; Enigma works like a polyalphabetic cipher whose key is repeated after 17,576 characters are encrypted. As long as the messages were shorter than that, frequency analysis would not work. Messages were actually much shorter: the maximum length of the messages, according to the instruction manual of one of its versions, was 250 letters.[16]

Finding the key was made more difficult by the fact that there were not just three rotors but rather five, out of which three were selected. The selected rotors could be put in any order that specified which would be the first, second, and third. All in all, the key of the Enigma depended on the rotors that were selected; their order in the machine; for the first two rotors, the position of a notch that affected the stepping of the next rotor; the initial starting position of each rotor; and the plugboard substitutions. All of these combine to give a total number of keys of about 10^{23}. Clearly, brute force would not work.[17]

It took the genius of Alan Turing to break the Enigma during the war, when he worked in the Government Code and Cypher School in Bletchley Park, north of London. Turing (1912–1954) was an English mathematician who did groundbreaking work in computer science, logic, and theoretical biology, apart from his work on cryptanalysis. His achievements are still with us today. In theoretical computer science, a *Turing machine* is a hypothetical device that defines what can and cannot be decided by a computer—any computer, no matter how powerful, now or in the future. He proposed the *Turing test* to determine when a machine will have become truly intelligent: when we fail to distinguish it from a human in a specific experimental setting where we conduct a dialogue with it. His instrumental role in breaking the Enigma was a state secret and remained unknown until the 1970s, while the full story did not emerge until the 1990s. Turing was not recognized during his lifetime for his contributions to the war effort, and in 1952, was convicted for homosexuality, which was then illegal in the United Kingdom.

His conviction entailed the removal of his security clearance. He was given a choice to either go to jail or undergo hormonal therapy for "chemical castration," and chose the latter. He was found dead two years later, with his death attributed to suicide. Turing was granted an official pardon posthumously in 2014.

But let us honor Turing by returning to his cryptanalysis. The Enigma decryption effort was an enormous achievement, not just because of its strategic importance, but because it made clear how cryptography would proceed from that point onward.

A key observation in breaking the Enigma was that most of the complexity of the key came from the plugboard settings, and this could be swept away because the plugboard is completely symmetric. Therefore, if two Enigma machines are connected one after the other, with the output of the first being the input of the second, the effects of the plugboard cancel out: in effect, it is taken out of the picture. You only have to check the different rotor possibilities.

Then Turing noticed that it was possible to test the rotor settings automatically, provided you had a piece of ciphertext and the corresponding piece of plaintext; this is called a *crib*. For example, in figure 17, you might know that WETTER (a common word in meteorological reports) was encrypted as ETJWPX in a message.

Having a crib means that you have at hand both the problem (the ciphertext) and solution (the plaintext). That

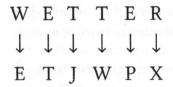

W E T T E R
↓ ↓ ↓ ↓ ↓ ↓
E T J W P X

Figure 17

is called a *known-plaintext attack*. Even if we do not know how to get from the problem to the solution, we can use cribs to crack the decryption method. When searching for the decryption key, instead of enumerating all possibilities, the correspondence between the crib plaintext and ciphertext can guide us through the search.

So it was with Enigma. If you come across a crib in which a plaintext letter occurs later in the ciphertext, like the letter *W* above, it means that you have an Enigma machine that encrypts *W* to *E*, then the rotors step forward to encrypt *E* to *T*, then they step forward again to encrypt *T* to *J*, and then again they step forward to encrypt *T* to *W*.

With a crib like that, you can take three Enigma machines and connect them one after the other, and the last one with the first, forming a loop. You can then set them so that the second Enigma machine is one step ahead of the first, and the third Enigma machine is two steps ahead of the second (there are two *T*s in WETTER). If you get the right rotor settings, an input of *W* to the first Enigma machine will give an output of *W* from the last

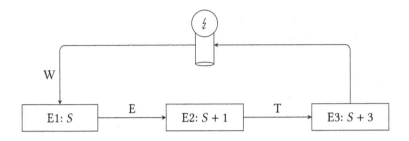

Figure 18

Enigma machine; by connecting all of them together, a circuit will close. In the following figure we indicate the position of the first Enigma machine with S, and the other two with $S + 1$ and $S + 3$, following the pattern we identified from the crib.

These ideas were put into practice by Turing in a machine called a *bombe*.[18] The bombe emulated connected Enigma machines working in parallel, like in figure 18, and tried different rotor settings until a circuit closed. Then the key was found. Initially, days were required for breaking a key. Turing incorporated improvements by Gordon Welchman, another mathematician working in Bletchley Park, into his designs. The improvements cut the decipher time to hours; Enigma was broken.[19]

Enigma was a turning point in cryptography. It was a *machine* that encrypted messages, and it took a *machine* to break it. From that point on, all cryptography would be carried out by machines. Even though both the Enigma and the bombe used to break it were electromechanical devices, once digital computers could be used for cryptographic purposes there was no turning back; nowadays, all cryptography is carried out by computers. The challenge is to design methods of encryption that are run by computers and are too difficult to break, even with the best computers at the adversaries' disposal. In the next chapter, we will see how we can do that today.

SYMMETRIC CRYPTOGRAPHY

Encryption is not unlike locking our secrets with a key; normally, we use the same key for both securing and opening a given lock. In cryptography, this translates to using the same key for encrypting a message and decrypting its encryption. If decryption of the message is possible with the possession of the same key used for encryption, then the whole scheme is called *symmetric encryption*, or symmetric cryptography. It is as if we lock our message in an unbreakable box, whose lock cannot be pried open unless we have the key with which we locked it.

That being said, when an appellation is given to describe a particular configuration, like using the same key for encryption and decryption, one is likely to suspect there may also be alternatives; after all, if using the same key for encryption and decryption were the only possibility, then all encryption would be symmetric and the adjective would be superfluous. The suspicion is warranted, as we will see in the following chapter. But for the time being, let's go back for a while to Victorian Britain.

Charles Dickens's Key

At one point in Dickens's first novel, *The Pickwick Papers*, Mr. Pickwick makes his way to his attorney, Mr. Perker. Having arrived early and found Perker's chambers closed, he waits until Perker's clerk, Mr. Lowten, arrives and greets him, "drawing a Bramah key from his pocket" to open the door. Then he "re-pocketed his Bramah." A "Bramah key"? Also previously in the book, another character complains about a pressing female acquaintance that "if I was locked up in a fire-proof chest with a patent Brahmin [i.e., Bramah], she'd find means to get at me."[1]

We know that "Dickens himself was not above 'advertizing' goods and services that pleased him."[2] And he had a fine eye for detail; Mr. Lowten could just as well have produced any key from his pocket and a chest could be locked with any other lock. What, then, is the Bramah key, and why did it earn its place inside the novel?

Joseph Bramah (1748–1814) was an English inventor during the Industrial Revolution. His most important invention was the hydraulic press, but his creativity ranged from inventing a water closet to beer brewing and paper manufacturing. In 1784, he got a patent for a lock and established the Bramah locks company in London. The Bramah lock was billed as pickproof. To stress the point, the company put up what came to be called the "Challenge Lock" on the window of its shop in 1790. The lock bore an inscription that read, "The Artist who can make an Instrument that will pick or Open this Lock, shall Receive 200 Guineas The Moment it is produced." You can see the Bramah lock with the inscription in figure 19.[3]

Despite the substantial prize—200 guineas being equivalent to about $33,082 in 2024 if we adjust for inflation, the challenge stood until a US locksmith, Alfred Charles Hobbs, managed to open the lock during the Great Exhibition of 1851. As reported by the *Economist* at the time, "THE LOCK CONTROVERSY.—The American picklock, Mr. Hobbs, has accomplished the picking and opening of the Bramah's patent lock, and the arbitrators have issued their report awarding him the 200 guineas."[4] It appears that the Victorians followed the developments closely; according to a newspaper report, nothing in the Great Exhibition attracted greater public attention than the lock contest. At stake was what lock manufacturers of the time advertised as "perfect security": a lock that could not be picked by thieves by any means possible. Bramah's lock had for decades remained inviolable until Hobbs divested from it the mantle of perfect security. Nevertheless, the quest for perfect security remained active, and

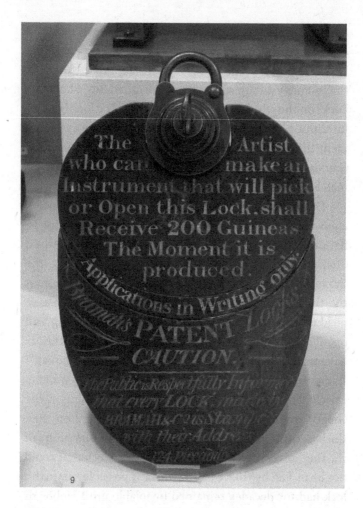

The   Artist
who cann   make an
Instrument that will pick
or Open this Lock, shall
Receive 200 Guineas
The Moment it is
produced.

Applications in Writing only

Bramah's PATENT Locks.

— CAUTION —

The Public is Respectfully Informed
that every LOCK made by
BRAMAH & Co is Stamped
with their Address
[illegible]

9

Figure 19

lock-picking competitions were a popular fixture of Victorian Britain.[5]

There is a detail in the Bramah challenge that we should not miss. The lock itself was, of course, a closed box, yet the mechanism of the lock was not a secret. Bramah had patented his lock and also described its design in "A Dissertation on the Construction of Locks," published in 1785. Confident in his design, and perhaps distressed at the prevailing state of affairs in lock security, in 1798 he wrote a petition to the House of Commons asking for an extension of his patent (which had a duration of fourteen years).[6]

Kerckhoffs's Principle

The story to this point cues us to an important feature of secure systems. A system's security should not depend on the fact that we don't know how it works. *A system should remain impregnable even if we know exactly how it works.* The idea that something is secure because we don't know how it is secured is a fallacy called "security by obscurity." If that something depends on a secret design, then once this is exposed or leaked, all guarantees are gone.

On the contrary, take a mechanism that we understand completely, yet even so we cannot break it despite our having full knowledge of its internal workings.

A system should remain impregnable even if we know exactly how it works. The idea that something is secure because we don't know how it is secured is a fallacy called "security by obscurity."

Wouldn't you trust that mechanism more than any other one that would ask you to trust that it works, magically but opaquely, although anything could happen once the veil is taken away? Hobbs, the locksmith who broke the Bramah lock, put it down eloquently: "Rogues are very keen in their profession, and know already much more than we can teach them respecting their several kinds of roguery."[7] Let us while away a bit longer in the nineteenth century to meet August Kerckhoffs (1835–1903), a Dutch linguist and cryptographer. In 1883, Kerckhoffs published two articles that changed the course of cryptography; in these, he enunciated six principles that, he argued, should guide cryptographic systems. The second of the six principles remains as relevant today as when it was published, and goes thus: "The system should not require secrecy, and falling into the enemy's hands should not pose an inconvenience." He went on the explain exactly what he meant by secrecy as "that which constitutes the material part of the system: tables, dictionaries, or whatever mechanical devices that are required for its operation."[8] In a lock, all of its security should reside in the possession of the key, not ignorance of its manufacture. Similarly, all security of a cryptographic system should reside in the key that is used for the encryption; no other assumption should be made about the confidentiality of its design.

A Lock Competition, Redux

Fast-forward to January 2, 1997, when the National Institute of Standards and Technology (NIST) of the United States announced a competition for "an unclassified, publicly disclosed encryption algorithm capable of protecting sensitive government information well into the next century."[9]

This is reminiscent of the lock-picking competitions of more than a hundred years before. People were invited to submit their mechanisms, here cryptographic algorithms, whose security and resilience would be examined openly by the cryptographic community. There would be no secrecy in the design itself. Following Kerckhoffs, the security of the messages encrypted with the new standard should reside entirely in the secrecy of the key used to encrypt them.

In 1997, there was already a data encryption standard in place, conveniently called the Data Encryption Standard (DES). It had been developed by IBM and was approved as a standard twenty years prior in 1977. DES, however, had not been keeping up with advances in computing power. There was concern by 1997 that DES could be broken using the computers of the day. In particular, people feared that it was becoming more and more possible to find the key with which a message was encoded and therefore decrypt it.

DES worked by taking a message to be encrypted and a key. Using the key, DES changed the message in a way that, it was hoped, became entirely unintelligible. The only way to recover the original message would be to use the key and feed it back to DES in order to decrypt the encryption.

The DES key was 56 bits long. If an attacker had no knowledge whatsoever of the key, they had to guess it. Unless they possessed Delphic powers, they would have to start trying possible keys, feeding each one of them to DES, until they recovered the original message. This was of course a brute-force attack, similar to what a burglar who knows nothing about safes would do: try all combinations of the safe's key until the safe opens.

That is feasible as long as the number of possible combinations for a key is low. Locksmiths know that; the importance of prohibiting a brute-force attack was not lost on Bramah when he was designing his own lock. In the petition he submitted to the House of Commons, he had included a table with the "number of changes"—that is, the permutations—for a given number of wafers in the lock. If a lock picker embarked on a brute-force attack on the Bramah lock, they would need to forge millions and millions of keys.

In DES, the number of possible keys was $2^{56} = 72,057,594,037,927,936$, more than 72 quadrillion. It is easy to see how we arrive at this number. The logic is the same with the calculations for deriving the number of operations needed to break the one-time pad. If we have a key that is composed of 1 bit, it can be either 0 or 1, so we have two possibilities. If the key is composed of 2 bits, the first bit can be 0 or 1, so two possibilities, while the second bit can also be 0 or 1, making two possibilities for each possible value of the first bit, or $2 \times 2 = 2^2 = 4$. If the key is composed of three bits, there are three possibilities for each bit, so in total $2 \times 2 \times 2 = 2^3$. For DES, we have $\overbrace{2 \times 2 \times \cdots \times 2}^{56} = 2^{56}$.

The concern on the weakness of a 56-bit key was well founded. Indeed, a challenge was set up offering a \$10,000 reward for breaking a DES-encrypted message. The gauntlet was taken up by a group of computer scientists called DESCHALL (for DES Challenge), which managed to decrypt the message harnessing the computing power of thousands of computers connected over the internet (in the end, 78,000 computers took part in the DESCHALL project). The project was announced on February 18, 1997. After trying nearly 18 quadrillion keys, the secret message was found on June 17: "Strong cryptography makes the world a safer place."[10] From that point, things deteriorated fast for DES. In 1998, the nonprofit Electronic Frontier Foundation (EFF) built a \$250,000 machine, called the EFF DES cracker (aka Deep Crack, after IBM's Deep Blue chess computer). Deep Crack won another challenge by breaking a DES message in fifty-six hours.

Not only was the decision to use a short key short-sighted, having failed to factor in advances in computing power. Parts of the design process of DES, and the rationale behind them, were kept under wraps. Working behind the scenes contravenes Kerckhoffs's principle: even if the design of a system is known, we must also know the why, not only the how. Worse, there were suspicions that particular design choices, far from contributing to the system's overall security, could actually harbor a *backdoor*—that is, a way to break the system without having to compromise the key. No small part of these suspicions was due to the fact that the National Security Agency (NSA) was involved in the design of DES. The NSA is, among other things, responsible for global data monitoring and collecting for the United States. It was therefore not paranoid to doubt the integrity of a secret system that had the blessing of an actor that would gain from being able to bypass, for its own advantage, the protections offered by the system.

It seems, from what we have learned since, that the NSA's contribution in the design of DES was double edged. On the one hand, the NSA hardened DES by improving details in its design so as to be able to withstand a certain kind of cryptographic attack, *differential cryptanalysis*, which was known to NSA and independently to IBM, but not to the wider cryptographic community. In differential cryptanalysis, we try to exploit the way different plaintexts lead to different ciphertexts. It turned out that DES was surprisingly resistant to differential cryptanalysis. On the other hand, the NSA recommended that DES should have a shorter key instead of the initial proposal of 64 bits. That would allow breaking DES with substantial, but not insurmountable, computing power, as indeed happened with the 56-bit key.

The Advanced Encryption Standard

We will probably never know whether the design of DES was tainted intentionally; be that as it may, the open competition for the successor to DES won nothing but praise from the worldwide cryptographic community, both for the conduct of the competition and for the final result. In the end, the winner was a cipher submitted by two Belgian cryptographers, Vincent Rijmen and Joan Daemen. The cipher was originally called Rijndael, after the names of its inventors, but has since been known as the Advanced Encryption Standard (AES). It still protects much of digital communications today.[11]

Figure 20 depicts what AES looks like.

Let's go through the figure to provide a condensed description of AES; we will give more details as we proceed. AES takes the plaintext message and breaks it into little pieces, called *blocks*, that are 16 bytes, equal to 128 bits, long. Each block is treated as a table that has 4 rows of

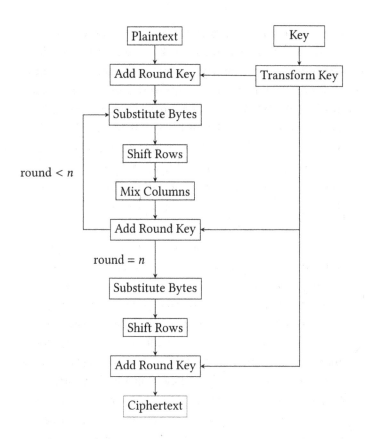

Figure 20

4 bytes each. It undergoes encryption and then AES proceeds to encrypt the next block. To encrypt each block, AES processes it in multiple *rounds*. The number of rounds varies depending on the length of the key we use, which can be 128, 192, or 256 bits long: 10 rounds for 128-bit keys, 12 rounds for 192-bit keys, and 14 rounds for 256-bit keys. In each round, the original key is transformed in some particular way and used to alter the plaintext block. Then the result of the transformation of the block using the round key undergoes a series of further transformations. In the first of them, we substitute each byte of the block with another byte, according to a specific substitution table. Then we take the resulting block, which, remember, we treat as a table, and shift its rows, again in a particular way. Having done that, we turn our attention to the columns, which we mix in a (you guessed it) particular way. Once we have done all of our rounds, we do another byte substitution, followed by row shifting, and before we produce the final ciphertext we add another key transformation. Decryption using AES is almost the same as encryption; the ciphertext undergoes a similar series of operations, doing the same number of rounds, until at the end all the mangling performed by the encryption is undone and the original plaintext block emerges on the output.

All of this looks rather mysterious, but we can get a better understanding of AES by peering into the distinct stages. This will also allow us to appreciate that AES is a careful choreography of steps, each chosen thoughtfully. Bear with us. It is worth pursuing the thread of AES in order to understand how a modern cryptographic method really works!

AES is based on two fundamental ideas of cryptography that had been introduced several decades before. In 1945, at the close of World War II, Claude Shannon (1916–2001), a mathematician and electrical engineer, wrote a classified memorandum developing "a mathematical theory of secret systems." A declassified version of the memorandum was published after the war, in 1949.[12] Shannon's contribution to cryptography was a small part of his achievements. He founded the field of information theory—that is, the mathematical study of digital information. The very word "bit," which stands for *binary digit*, was proposed by Shannon. He completed his master's thesis at MIT at the age of twenty-three; in the thesis, he showed that electric circuits could implement Boolean algebra, which is one of the foundations of digital computers. Shannon also explored computer chess, juggled and unicycled, and was the coinventor (with mathematician Edward O. Thorp) of the first wearable computer, whose purpose was to beat the casino at roulette.

In the memorandum, Shannon proposed that a cryptographic system should employ two methods for ensuring secrecy. The first is *diffusion*, which "dissipates" the statistical properties of the plaintext among "long-range statistics" of the ciphertext. Recall that we can break a ciphertext by exploiting its statistical properties, like letter frequencies. Such an attack could be thwarted if we have each letter in the input plaintext influence many letters in the output ciphertext. Then there would be no direct correspondence between the frequencies of the ciphertext and those of the plaintext: the frequencies of the input would be diffused among the output. Ideally, we would like the value of one bit in the input plaintext to affect half the bits of the output plaintext. That is an instance of the *avalanche effect* in cryptography: a slight change in the input should result in significant changes in the output.

The second method that Shannon proposed is *confusion*, which should make the relationship between the statistical properties of the ciphertext and encryption key as complex as possible. In this way, it will not be possible to find the key by exploiting ciphertexts.

We can see how confusion and diffusion are applied in practice in the way AES gets from the plaintext to the ciphertext. As we said, AES works with blocks of bits taken together; it is therefore a *block cipher*. When given some data to encrypt, it slices up the data into chunks, the blocks, of 16 bytes each, equal to 128 bits. If there are fewer than 16 bytes available to make a block (i.e., the number of bytes in the data is not a multiple of 16), it pads the block with 0s. The 16 bytes in a block are arranged in

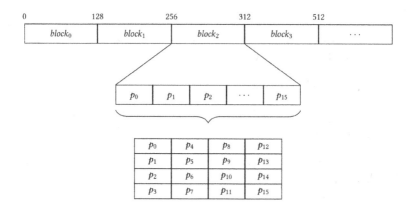

Figure 21

a matrix—that is, a table, which is called the *state*; see figure 21, where individual bytes of the plaintext are written with $p_0, p_1, \ldots, p_{15}$.

The first step in AES is to add to the state a subkey (the round key) that is derived from the encryption key. The addition is performed using the exclusive-or (XOR, $\oplus$) operation. XOR works on individual bits: if either, but not both, of 2 bits are 1, the result is 1; otherwise it is 0, as depicted in figure 22.

The state and subkey are processed bit by bit; each bit of each byte of the state is XORed with the corresponding bit of the corresponding byte of the subkey. Then the state contains a new set of 16 bytes, $x_0, x_1, \ldots, x_{15}$. Characters are represented in computers as numbers according to

x	y	$x \oplus y$
0	0	0
1	0	1
0	1	1
1	1	0

Figure 22

standard *character encodings*. These numbers are in their turn represented as bits grouped in bytes. Suppose that one of the bytes of the state contains the character *N*, which inside a computer is represented as the number 78 with the sequence of bits 01001110 in binary. If the sub-key gives us the character *o*, represented as the number 111 with the sequence of bits 01101111, then we have:

```
  01001110
⊕ 01101111
  ─────────
  00100001
```

The resulting bits 00100001, equal to the number 33, are the internal representation of the character *!* in the computer. That is, the *N* of the state, given *o* from the sub-key, will be transformed to *!*, as shown in figure 23.

p_0	p_4	p_8	p_{12}
p_1	p_5	p_9	p_{13}
p_2	p_6	p_{10}	p_{14}
p_3	p_7	p_{11}	p_{15}

$\oplus$
XOR

k_0	k_4	k_8	k_{12}
k_1	k_5	k_9	k_{13}
k_2	k_6	k_{10}	k_{14}
k_3	k_7	k_{11}	k_{15}

x_0	x_4	x_8	x_{12}
x_1	x_5	x_9	x_{13}
x_2	x_6	x_{10}	x_{14}
x_3	x_7	x_{11}	x_{15}

Figure 23

AES then proceeds by combining both confusion and diffusion. To create confusion, AES substitutes the bytes in the state by special values. This is done using a look-up table called an *S-box* (for substitution box). There are $2^8 = 256$ different bytes, so the S-box contains 256 values, one for each possible byte value. AES takes each byte of the state and substitutes it with the value found in the corresponding position of the S-box. For instance, suppose that character *B* is stored in one of the bytes of the state. AES looks up *B* in the S-box and finds that it should be substituted by the character ;. The *B* in the state is thus changed to ;, and similarly for all other bytes in the state, as seen in figure 24.

Having substituted the contents of the state according to the S-box, AES applies diffusion by permuting and mixing the data in the state. It permutes the contents of

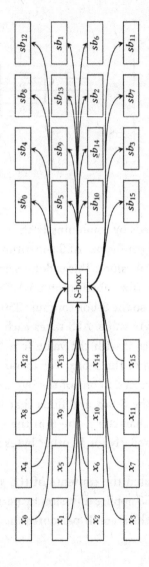

Figure 24

all rows except the first by shifting them leftward one, two, and three positions, respectively, wrapping around the left end of each row of the state. This wrapping around explains why in figure 25, sb_{11}, for instance, moves one place to the right; it actually moves three places to the left, and when it reaches the left end, it comes back from the right end. But this would create a mess of arrows in the figure.

After the contents of the rows are shifted, AES mixes up the contents of each column, applying a mathematical transformation to its bytes and producing a new column; see figure 26.

Following the mixing of the columns, another sub-key is added to the current state, as in the first step, completing a round. As we said, each block of plaintext goes through at least ten rounds, one after the other (only in the last round are columns not mixed). At the end of the final round, we get the final ciphertext.

What about decryption? Once we have encrypted our data with AES, how can we recover the original plaintext, given the plaintext? The operations carried out by AES are reversible provided we have the original encryption key. Given the encryption key and ciphertext, we follow a similar suite of operations (with some changes; for instance, we use an inverse S-box for substituting bytes) that undo the changes, dispel the confusion, and tidy up the diffusion.

The steps inside a round appear as a feast of slicing, dicing, and mixing the plaintext—they have probably made

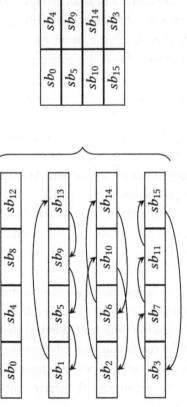

Figure 25

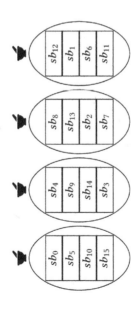

Figure 26

you lose track of what is happening—and we do that several times. There also seems to be some magic involved. What are the contents of the S-box that dictate how bytes are substituted? And what about the mathematical operation that mixes up the contents of each column of the state?

Rijmen and Daemen did not arrive at this slicing, dicing, and mixing at random. The contents of the S-box are chosen carefully, following mathematical properties that ensure that the results of the byte substitution step are resistant to cryptanalysis. The operation performed when mixing the columns is a special form of matrix multiplication of each column. The operation has again been chosen carefully so as to provide a good deal of diffusion in the cipher.

Following Enigma and the mechanization of cryptography, a good cipher should be able to withstand sustained attacks where the adversary may possess large amounts of computing power. It is difficult, therefore, for a good cipher to be the fruit of dilettante effort. If we expect computers and algorithms to attack our cipher, then the cipher had better have the best guarantees that it can withstand such attacks. Such guarantees are provided by mathematics. Good ciphers have strong mathematical foundations.

The particular way that rows are shifted, columns are mixed, and bytes are substituted is determined by operations that have been chosen to ensure that the resulting ciphertext looks random, and that it is not possible to establish any relationships between the ciphertext and the original plaintext. The operations follow principles of *number theory* to ensure that.

That is another characteristic of modern cryptography. Whereas traditional cryptography is mostly a matter of substituting and mixing alphabets, in modern cryptography we treat everything as a number (to a computer even text is a series of numbers, so that is no problem). We want to transform the plaintext numbers in such a way that recovering them is infeasible without knowledge of the key. To be sure that these transformations are indeed capable of doing that, we usually rely on the arithmetic properties of the numbers, and number theory is the field of mathematics that deals with that.

Number theory has long been held as a mathematician's playground. It is the study of numbers themselves, without (at least as was thought) any immediate applications. Take, for instance, British mathematician G. H. Hardy, who in 1940 wrote an essay, "A Mathematician's Apology," extolling the beauty of mathematics independent of practical uses. He had something particular to say for number theory:

> If the theory of numbers could be employed for
> any practical and obviously honorable purpose, if
> it could be turned directly to the furtherance of
> human happiness or the relief of human suffering,
> as physiology and even chemistry can, then surely

Whereas traditional cryptography is mostly a matter of substituting and mixing alphabets, in modern cryptography we treat everything as a number.

neither [Carl Friedrich] Gauss nor any other mathematician would have been so foolish as to decry or regret such applications. But science works for evil as well as for good (and particularly, of course, in time of war); and both Gauss and lesser mathematicians may be justified in rejoicing that there is one science at any rate, and that their own, whose very remoteness from ordinary human activities should keep it gentle and clean.[13]

As we'll see time and again in this book, Gauss and his lesser colleagues would no longer have reason to rejoice.

AES is built on good foundations, but that is not enough. There may still have been something that its inventors missed—some weak link in the sequence of encryption operations of which they were not aware. That is where the initial competition entered the scene: the cryptographic community agreed that, to its best knowledge, AES is good. Perhaps more important, that verdict has stood the test of time. Since the adoption of AES, many people have examined the cipher and tried to find chinks in its construction. To this day, we don't know of any practical, successful cryptanalysis attacks against AES. AES is secure, fast, and open.

We can get a glimpse of the power of AES by a simple example. Let's take the following image of a key in figure 27. The image has dimensions $16 \times 8 = 128$; each square in the grid corresponds to 1 bit that is either 0 or 1, so the image has 16 bytes and can fit in a single AES block. If we encrypt the contents of the image using AES, we get the image in figure 28, which arguably bears no resemblance to the original image.

Let's now add a tooth to the key; if you notice carefully, you will see it on the top of the blade in figure 29. This is the smallest change we can make to our plaintext; it corresponds to flipping just one bit. If we encrypt the contents of the altered image, we get the new ciphertext image in figure 30, which looks very different from the ciphertext of the original image.

By comparing the two ciphertexts, we can determine how different they actually are. Of the 128 bits of each ciphertext, only 57 are the same. A change of a single bit in the plaintext created a cascade of 71 changes in the ciphertext. That is 55 percent. We have already mentioned the avalanche effect. A formal definition of the effect is the strict avalanche criterion, which requires that an average of half of the output bits should change when a single input bit is changed. We see that AES gets there.[14]

Modes of Operation and Authentication

Although in our particular example AES does a good job of hiding the original image, in practice AES as we described it may not be good enough. The reason is that if

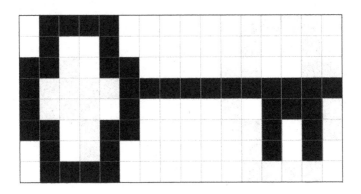

Figure 27

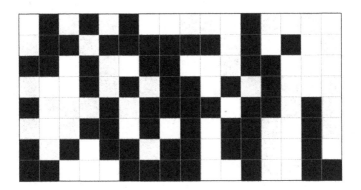

Figure 28

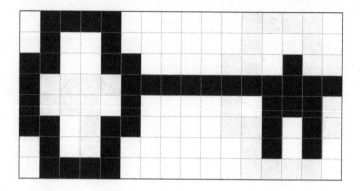

Figure 29

Figure 30

the plaintext contains two identical blocks of data, these will be encrypted to the same ciphertext. AES is deterministic: identical inputs will produce the same output. You can see the problem in the encryption of the image of Felix the Cat in figure 31.[15] To encrypt the image, AES will take chunks of 16 bytes each; however, most of the chunks will be identical blocks of white or black pixels. They will thus be encrypted to identical ciphertexts. This will result in the encrypted image in figure 32, showing a visible trace of the original image. This is clearly not what we want to see. We want to see something like the image in figure 33.

It appears that despite our assertions about the security of AES, we are back to square one, as under the right circumstances it would be trivial to deduce information on the plaintext from the ciphertext. AES, however, has different *modes* of operation, which build on the basic flow that we have described. The bare-bones mode, which takes each block and encrypts it independently of the others, is called the *electronic code book* (ECB) *mode*. You can see it diagrammatically below in figure 34, taking each block of plaintext (P_0, P_1, . . .) and the key K to produce the ciphertexts (C_0, C_1, . . .); decryption is simply the other way around, shown in figure 35. ECB is not used in practice, for the very reason we have just discussed.

Other modes ensure that each block is encrypted differently, even if it is identical to other blocks. In the *cipher block chaining* (CBC) *mode*, each block of plaintext is first

Figure 31

Figure 32

Figure 33

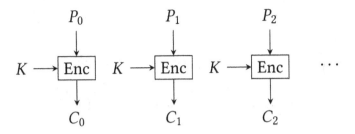

Figure 34

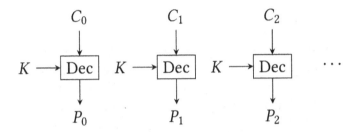

Figure 35

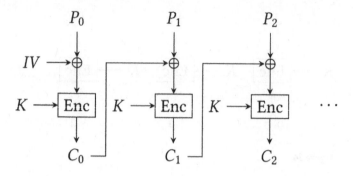

Figure 36

XORed with the previous ciphertext block and then en-crypted. Hence the encryption of each block depends on the history of the encryption of the previous blocks. CBC encryption and decryption are depicted in figures 36–37. For the first block, for which we have no previous one, we use a random sequence of bits called *initialization vector* (IV) in its place.

Another mode, the *counter (CTR) mode*, uses the key to encrypt an arbitrary number, called a *nonce*, and a counter; then it takes their encrypted output and XORs it with each block of plaintext. In figures 38–39, note that the key is applied to the nonce and the counter, not to the plaintext as before. As the counter changes with each block, no two plaintext blocks, even identical ones, will be encrypted to the same ciphertext. The nonce, which is random, guaran-tees that each time AES is run, the whole ciphertext will

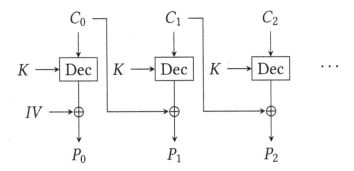

Figure 37

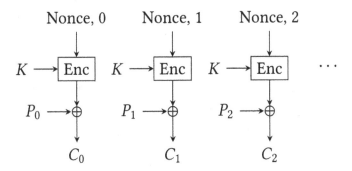

Figure 38

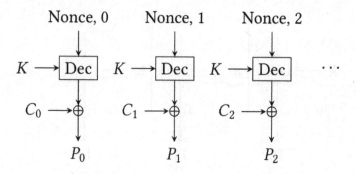

Figure 39

be different, even though the whole plaintext may be the same, and the counter may start each time from zero. Another advantage of CTR over CBC is that the encrypted data can be partially decrypted even if some part has been corrupted or lost; in CBC mode, even a single flipped bit in the beginning will make all ciphertext unusable.

Using AES with the CTR mode on our Felix the Cat example produces the encrypted image in figure 33, which we wanted to see. That image looks random and shows no traces of the original.

Apart from the extra security, CTR offers another feature. As it uses the key to encrypt the nonce and the counter, it produces a continuous stream of encrypted data (encrypted nonce and counter blocks), which, thanks to the good offices of AES, appears to be random. This random stream is XORed byte by byte with the plaintext.

A cipher that works by combining plaintext bytes with a pseudorandom stream of bytes is called a *stream cipher*. A stream cipher harks back to the one-time pad, and it would be a one-time pad if the stream of bytes combined with the plaintext were truly random. It is not—AES is deterministic, after all. But it is an excellent pseudorandom stream.

A stream cipher can encrypt data of any size, and does not require the plaintext to align with blocks or pad with zeroes. Moreover, it can encrypt data on the fly, as it comes, without waiting for whole blocks. For example, video and sound in popular conferencing and calling applications travel as data streams. These streams are usually encrypted using AES running CTR or some other mode that turns them into stream ciphers. Encryption and decryption using AES is fast, so we do not notice any delay; when the quality of our encrypted video call is bad, it is a result of slow network data transmission, not of the overhead placed by encryption and decryption.

Confidentiality and Authenticity

With a good symmetric encryption algorithm, like AES, we can achieve *confidentiality* in our communications. But this is not always enough. Even though we may be confident that our messages will remain secret, a different threat lurks. Suppose we have a malicious actor that, although not able to read our messages, is able to *alter* them. A malicious attacker is usually called Mallory; unlike Eve the eavesdropper, who can only intercept messages, Mallory can change, substitute, or replay messages. Mallory does not need to know the plaintext to do that. He could intercept the ciphertexts en route to their destination and directly change their contents by altering the bits and bytes that constitute them.

This is the way a *chosen ciphertext attack* works. Mallory is able to obtain the decryption, or at least some information about the decryption, of ciphertexts of his choice. If he has knowledge of chosen ciphertexts and their corresponding plaintexts, he can carefully craft a ciphertext that decrypts to a desired plaintext. For instance, he may know that a given ciphertext is an order to transfer a certain amount of money. By altering that ciphertext, he may be able to produce a new ciphertext that is again a transfer order but for a different amount of money. It is not an exotic possibility. The CTR mode is vulnerable to chosen ciphertext attacks.

All of this shows that, in addition to confidentiality, there is another desideratum for our communication systems: *authenticity*. We need to be sure that the messages that we receive are the authentic ones that were meant to reach us, entirely unadulterated. Cryptographers have bent their minds on the problem and devised ways to guarantee authenticity as well as confidentiality. Conveniently for us, one way to achieve both relies on yet another mode of operation that combines two of the modes of cipher operation that we have seen. Instead of sending only the encrypted message, we sent the ciphertext accompanied by a short piece of information, called a *tag* or *message authentication code* (MAC), which uniquely identifies the original plaintext. The idea is that the recipient, after decrypting the message, can verify that the received MAC corresponds to the plaintext. If it does not, the ciphertext has been altered.

To construct the MAC, the plaintext M is encrypted using the CBC mode, but we keep only the encryption of the final block. This is our tag, which we denote by T in figure 40. To make sure that an attacker cannot forge the tag, the IV of the CBC mode is set to all zeros. If we don't

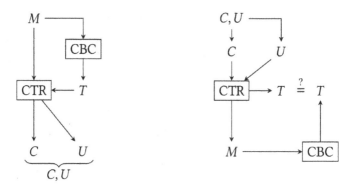

Figure 40

do that, the attacker could take a different first block that, with a properly chosen IV, could result in the same second block. The way CBC works, if we have the same second block, we'll get the same third block, and so on, until the same final block. The attacker would produce the same tag for the message with the altered first block.

From the way it is constructed, the tag is also called (little surprise here) *cipher block chaining message authentication code* (CBC-MAC). We then encrypt the plaintext using CTR mode to get the ciphertext C and also encrypt the tag T using CTR mode to get an encrypted tag U. At the end, we join the ciphertext C and encrypted tag U to form the final message that we will send.

The recipient reverses the process, starting by decrypting C and U using CTR mode. From the plaintext M, they derive the tag T using CBC mode and verify that the tag derived from the decrypted plaintext is the same as the tag derived by decrypting U. If at some point in transit the message was altered, it will produce a plaintext whose tag will not match the received tag. That is because *the tag depends on the original plaintext*, not on the ciphertext, as you can verify in the figure. Altering the ciphertext will result in decrypting a different plaintext, with a different tag. The whole sequence of events constitutes the *counter with cipher block chaining message authentication code mode*, or simply *CCM mode*. This mode assures us of both confidentiality and authenticity.

CCM operates in an *authenticate-then-encrypt* manner. Alternatively, we may use an *encrypt-then-authenticate* approach. Such an approach is adopted by the *Galois / counter mode* (GCM). The plaintext is encrypted using the CTR mode. The encrypted blocks are also used to produce an authentication tag. That is done using a special form of multiplication called *multiplication over a Galois field*, hence its name. Évariste Galois (1811–1832) was a French mathematician who died lamentably young, at age twenty, from wounds inflicted in a duel; before that he laid down the foundations of abstract algebra that today underpin much of modern mathematical cryptography.

Catch-22

AES obeys Kerckhoffs's principle; its internal workings are public knowledge and all secrecy resides with the key that is used for both the (symmetric) encryption and decryption. But then this begs the question, How is the key agreed on between the two parties that wish to communicate? We cannot send a key to our partner over the internet because Eve will be able to intercept it. Of course, we could encrypt it, but to encrypt the key we would need to agree on some other key that we would use to encrypt our AES key, and so on and so forth. We could send our key using a trusted courier, but this is not a practical approach. Or we could exchange a key using a secure communications channel, but if we had such a channel, perhaps we would not need encryption in the first place.

It is a catch-22 situation. We must give to our recipient the encrypted message and the key to decrypt it. If we give the key unencrypted, anybody intercepting it will be able to decrypt the message. If we give the key encrypted, the recipient will then not be able to decrypt the message because they will have to decrypt the key, yet they do not have the key to do *that*.

We are up against the *key exchange* or *key distribution problem*: How do we exchange the keys needed for secure encrypted communication? Unless we solve the key exchange problem, AES and any other symmetric encryption scheme cannot be used widely, and certainly not for secure, remote, digital communications. Because mechanisms such as trusted couriers or secure communication channels are beyond the means of most of us, private communication would have remained outside the reach of all but a few, such as spies, diplomats, and operatives. The solution of the key exchange problem, which really opened up cryptography for all, takes us to the next chapter.

KEY EXCHANGE AND PUBLIC
KEY CRYPTOGRAPHY

South of Hyde Park, in the Knightsbridge area of London, Brompton Oratory is a large Roman Catholic church built in the nineteenth century. Well-known people and aristocrats have married there, where religious ceremonies continue to be celebrated to this day. But churchgoers, passersby, and tourists (it is located right next to the Victoria and Albert Museum) may not be aware of its role in a different kind of ceremony that took place during the Cold War. The Brompton Oratory was used as a *dead drop* or *dead letter box* by Soviet spies in Britain.[1] A dead drop is a location where spies agree to exchange secret information. One agent leaves a secret item there, from where it is picked up by another agent later.

A dead drop is a solution to the key-exchange problem: the location is the means of exchange. Apart from its appeal as an echo of spy stories, it can have practical value when what we want to exchange is a material object. Still, there are obvious drawbacks. The location must remain secret and be communicated somehow in the first place. If it is compromised, apart from losing any value as a secret exchange mechanism, it can also be used to seed misinformation by counterintelligence agents placing fake material in the dead drop. And it certainly cannot be used on a large scale by people who want to keep their affairs private.

Today a dead drop of a different nature is a secure repository of digital documents, which is typically used to allow whistleblowing through the internet. Whistleblowers can communicate with investigative teams, such as journalists, without revealing their identity. Modern dead drops are used by prominent news organizations.

Back to the underlying problem, which we sketched at the end of the previous chapter: if we want to communicate securely, we must first establish a key that will secure our communication. Barring meeting face-to-face to exchange a key or using a dead drop to leave a key so that our recipient can then pick it up, what is there to do? In order to enable cryptography for the masses, the key exchange problem must be solved efficiently so that every one of us can establish and use secret keys for our everyday digital communications. The problem baffled cryptographers for a long time. On the face of it, it is not even obvious that a solution exists: to encrypt something, we need a secret key; to agree on a secret, we would need to communicate and encrypt it with some other secret key, and so on ad infinitum. And yet it can be done, and in this chapter we will see how.

Diffie-Hellman Key Exchange

We can understand how two people can agree on a secret key without a secure communications channel by using an analogy with paints.[2] Suppose we have Alice and Bob who want to agree on a common arbitrary color to use, but that will remain known only to them. They start by agreeing on a common base color—say, yellow. They agree on that common color publicly; for example, they just make an unencrypted call or exchange plain email messages. An interloper, Eve, will therefore know that they chose yellow. Next, Alice puts one liter of yellow on a three-liter pot and adds another liter of a different color, which she keeps secret. Bob does the same: in a three-liter pot, he puts one liter of yellow and another liter of some other color that he keeps secret. Both Alice and Bob mix the contents of their pots thoroughly. At this point, Alice's pot contains a paint whose color is a mixture of yellow and her secret color. Similarly, Bob's pot contains a paint whose color is a mixture of yellow and his secret color. Alice sends her pot to Bob, and Bob sends his pot to Alice. When Alice gets Bob's pot, she adds to it a liter of her secret color and mixes it thoroughly. Now the pot in Alice's hands contains a mixture of yellow, her secret color, and Bob's secret color. Bob does exactly the same: once he gets Alice's pot, he adds a liter of his own secret color and ends up with a pot containing a mixture of yellow, his secret color, and Alice's secret color. That means that both Alice and Bob have pots with the same color. That color is a secret known only to them. Why? Because even if Eve intercepts the pots as they travel between Alice and Bob, she cannot reverse the mixture to arrive at the original colors used to produce it: yellow and Alice's or Bob's secret color. The final color is also arbitrary: neither Alice nor Bob can know beforehand what the final color will be.

The original color, yellow, is publicly known. The mixture of yellow and Alice's secret color can also be publicly known, but as long as it cannot be unmixed, Alice's secret color will remain known only to Alice. In the same way, even though the mixture of yellow and Bob's secret color can be publicly known, as long as it cannot be unmixed, Bob's secret color will not be known by anybody else. So once Alice adds her secret color to Bob's mix, and Bob adds his secret color to Alice's mix, they will both get the same resulting mix, but nobody else will be able to arrive at the same mix from the pots that have been exchanged. Thus Alice and Bob have managed to agree on a secret, even though no part of their communication was secret.

In reality, we do not want a color for a cryptographic key; our key will be a number. So we need a method with which Alice and Bob will agree on a secret number by sending each other messages. All of these messages will be sent through an insecure channel, so an eavesdropper will know their content. And yet based on these messages, Alice and Bob will agree on a secret number that will not be discoverable by anybody else.

Let's see how such a scheme could work, step by step, translating from colors to numbers.

1. Alice and Bob agree on a common number (as they agreed on a common base color). Let's say that they agree on the number 2 and they do that in public, with no secrecy involved. The common number need not be that small, but it's more convenient for us here.

2. Alice and Bob each pick a number that they keep secret. Suppose that Alice picks 5 and Bob picks 8.

3. Alice mixes her secret number with the common number. To do that, she raises the common number to the power of her secret number: $2^5 = 32$. Bob mixes his secret number in the same way: $2^8 = 256$.

4. They send each other their results; again, this is not done in secret. Alice simply sends 32 in the open to Bob, and he sends 256 in the open to Alice.

5. Alice takes the number received from Bob and mixes it with her secret number. To mix, she raises it to the power

of her secret number. That is, $256^5 = 1,099,511,627,776$. Bob does exactly the same using his secret number: $32^8 = 1,099,511,627,776$.

With this sequence of mixes, they both arrive at the same number much like they arrived at the same color before. That is no coincidence. When we raise a number to a power and then to another power, we will get the same result if we raise the number first to the second power and then to the first. In mathematics, raising a number to a power is called the *exponentiation operation*. We call the number the *base* of the exponentiation and the power the *exponent*. A property of exponentiation is $(b^m)^n = (b^n)^m = b^{(mn)}$; raising a power of a number to a power is the same as raising the original number to the product of the two powers. Alice and Bob can therefore always use the above steps to calculate a shared number.

As such, we can generalize. We'll use g for the common number on which Alice and Bob agree at the start, a for Alice's secret number, and b for Bob's secret number. We can depict the steps and exchange of messages as in the following figure. We assume that the communication channel between Alice and Bob is not secure. Eve, an eavesdropper, knows everything that passes between Alice and Bob, as in figure 41.

Alice and Bob agree on a number g. Then Alice selects a random number a that she keeps secret. Bob also selects a

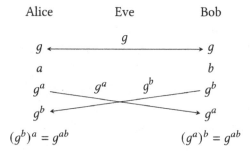

Figure 41

random number b that he keeps secret. Alice calculates g^a and sends it to Bob. Bob calculates g^b and sends it to Alice. Now Alice takes the number she received from Bob, g^b, and raises it to her secret number a, getting $(g^b)^a = g^{ab}$. Similarly, Bob takes the number he received from Alice, g^a, and raises it to his secret number b, getting $(g^a)^b = g^{ab}$.

Can they use that as their secret? Unfortunately not. In the paint-mixing example, we took it for granted that a paint mix cannot be unmixed. That is not true here. If Eve knows the common base number, g, and any of the numbers g^a and g^b that Alice and Bob exchange, she can immediately arrive at their shared secret. That is because exponentiation is a reversible operation. In the same way that subtraction is the inverse of addition and division is the inverse of multiplication, the inverse of exponentiation is the *logarithm* operation. If we raise b to the power of m, getting $y = b^m$, the base b logarithm of b^m is $\log_b y = m$. In our example, if Eve gets 2^5, sent by Alice to Bob, she can immediately inverse the exponentiation operation by taking its logarithm base 2: $\log_2 2^5 = 5$. Or if she gets 2^8, she can calculate $\log_2 2^8 = 8$. Knowing any of the secrets, Eve can use it as in step 5 above and arrive at the agreed-on, nonsecret number. In more general terms, if Eve knows g and g^a or g^b, she can immediately get $a = \log_g g^a$ or $b = \log_g g^b$ and then calculate g^{ab}.

The weakness in our scheme is that we have not used an irreversible mathematical operation equivalent to paint mixing. A mathematical operation, or to be more precise, a function that can easily compute a result given some input such that we cannot find the original input given the result, is called a *one-way function*. It is a function that mixes the input so that we cannot unmix it. One-way functions are a key component of cryptographic mechanisms and are strange beasts because we don't really know that they exist at all. Their existence remains an open conjecture. We know of functions that to the best of our knowledge produce outputs from which we cannot derive their inputs, but we don't know (yet) that some breakthrough will not happen and a mechanism won't be found that will transform one-way functions to two-way ones.

We need a way to transform the arithmetic operations that Alice and Bob perform into real mixing operations using one-way functions (or at least using what we believe are one-way functions). The key ingredient for doing that is modular arithmetic, which we encountered in the previous chapter. Recall that modular addition is simply adding two numbers and taking the remainder of the sum with the modulus. Modular arithmetic is not limited to addition. It also applies to multiplication: after multiplying two numbers, we take the remainder of the product with the modulus.

The modulus operation is the magic ingredient that will get us to the mixing operation we want. Instead of Alice and Bob simply raising their common number to some secret power, they will exponentiate *and then* will take the remainder of the division with another, nonsecret number. In other words, instead of using just exponentiation, they will use *modular exponentiation*.

Let's see what our previous sequence of steps will look like, as portrayed in figure 42.

1. Alice and Bob agree on a common number (as they agreed on a common base color). Let's say that they agree on the number $g = 2$ and do that in public, with no secrecy involved. They also agree on a prime number that will be their common modulus, which is not kept secret. We'll use p to denote the modulus. Suppose they pick $p = 227$ as the modulus.

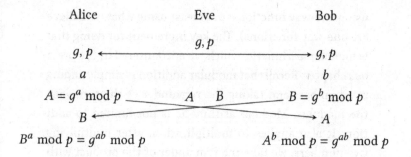

Figure 42

2. Alice and Bob each pick a number that they keep secret. Suppose that Alice picks $a = 17$ and Bob picks $b = 11$.

3. Alice mixes her secret number with the common number, *taking the remainder with the modulus*. To do that, she raises the common number to the power of her secret number, modulo 227. We'll use A to denote Alice's result, so we have $A = 2^{17} \bmod 227 = 93$. Bob mixes his secret number in the same way. We'll use B to denote Bob's result, so we have $B = 2^{11} \bmod 227 = 5$ (performing these calculations is straightforward using a computer).

4. They send each other their results; again, this is not done in secret. Alice simply sends $A = 93$ in the open to Bob, and he sends $B = 5$ to Alice, also in the open.

5. Alice takes the number received from Bob and mixes it with her secret number. To mix, she raises it to the power

of her secret number, modulo 227. That is, $A^b \bmod p = 5^{17} \bmod 227 = 194$. Bob does exactly the same using his secret number: $B^a \bmod p = 93^{11} \bmod 227 = 194$.

Alice and Bob calculate the same number again. This time, however, even if Eve has intercepted their common number $g = 2$, modulus $p = 227$, and the other messages, A and B, which Alice and Bob exchange, she cannot find Alice's and Bob's secret numbers and cannot determine that the common secret to which they arrived is the number 194. That is because as far as we know, there is no way to inverse modular exponentiation. That is called the *discrete logarithm problem*: if we have $g^x \bmod p$, we do not know an efficient way to find x, even if we know p and g. So Eve cannot find a or b, and therefore cannot find the shared value $g^{ab} \bmod p$.

We can get a visual idea of how modular exponentiation behaves like a one-way function. The exponential function behaves predictably, increasing at a frantic pace. You can see that in the left half of figure 43, where we have calculated the powers of 2 up to 100; they quickly grow beyond the borders of the figure, so we display the function $f(x) = 2^x$ on two different scales. The left y-axis is the normal scale, which we have to truncate to make it fit, and the right y-axis is a *logarithmic scale*. A logarithmic scale has values at intervals that grow exponentially (here, powers of 2) instead of linearly (multiples of a number). Exponential functions show up as straight lines on logarithmic scales.

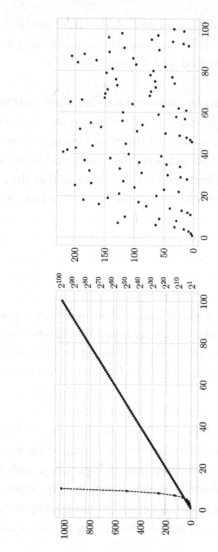

Figure 43

When a function $f(x)$ follows a clear pattern on a plot, it is usually easy to find the values of x that produce given values of $f(x)$—that is, it is easy to *invert* the function. In the case of the exponential function, it is trivial to invert it by taking its logarithm. This is in effect what the straight line in the left of figure 43 shows. You can find the value of x given 2^x by locating 2^x on the right scale and grabbing the x on the x-axis.

If we switch to the right side of figure 43, however, we see the function $f(x) = 2^x \bmod 227$. In lieu of a predictable, smooth plot, we get an erratic bunch of points. There does not appear to be any pattern to these points; if we did not know how they were produced, we might assume that they are random numbers. That is exactly the problem for Eve: she gets the $2^x \bmod 227$ values and is at a loss as to how to get the corresponding x values. She cannot take the logarithm of $2^x \bmod 227$, which would give her x. There are no other straight lines or patterns in the figure.

Whereas we can invert the function $f(x) = 2^x$, we cannot invert the function $f(x) = 2^x \bmod 227$, and this does not hold just for $g = 2$ and $p = 227$. Unless we are careless in our choice of g and p, we cannot invert the general function $f(x) = g^x \bmod p$—an illustration of why it is a one-way function.

This mechanism that allows Alice and Bob to exchange a key securely is called the *Diffie-Hellman key exchange*, after Whitfield Diffie and Martin Hellman, who published it in 1976, changing cryptography forever.[3] Up to that point, the cryptographic community did not have any practical solution to the key exchange problem. The Diffie-Hellman key exchange was the first method that allowed two people, no matter how far away from each other they are and how insecure their communication channel, to establish a truly secure shared key that they can then use with the encryption mechanism they want.

There is a way out for Eve: she can do a brute-force attack, trying different x values until she finds the correct one for a value $g^x \bmod p$. In our example, if she gets the value 93 from a wiretap, knowing $g = 2$ and $p = 227$, she can start calculating $2^x \bmod 227$ for $x = 1, 2, \ldots$ After a few tries, she will find that $2^{17} \bmod 227 = 93$, so she will have found the discrete logarithm. She will be able to do that only when the numbers are small, however, so we make sure that the numbers are not small at all. We make sure p is an enormous number, such as one with 4,096 bits or 1,234 decimal digits. We also make sure that a and b are big, such as 256 bits each—that is, 77 decimal digits. Brute force will not be a viable option. Eve will have to try a preposterous amount of numbers to find the right one. We used 227 here to make the case, but in real-world applications we use Diffie-Hellman with numbers that preempt the possibility of brute-force attacks.

You may wonder how we can perform calculations with numbers that are so big. Is Diffie-Hellman an efficient method? It is. There exist excellent algorithms for raising numbers to powers, performing many fewer calculations than we would need to by simply multiplying repeatedly as many times as the exponent indicates. Taking the remainder of the exponentiation is also something that we can do quickly. Although the calculations look frightening, they are in fact trifles for a computer.

There do exist some loopholes that would allow Eve to break the discrete logarithm problem. We do not know of any efficient way to solve it, but that does not mean that such a way will never be found. We do believe, though, that it is unlikely that we will find an easy solution. More devious are attacks that take advantage of the fact that the discrete logarithm problem is not *always* hard. If the parameters g and p are not chosen such that certain properties from number theory are satisfied, then there do exist algorithms to find the discrete logarithm more efficiently than brute force. To avoid that, we always choose g and p carefully. For instance, you may have noticed that the modulus p should be a prime number. The calculations in Diffie-Hellman work even if p is a composite, but that is not secure. In our choices, we should be following recommendations that are published openly. As long as we follow them, we know that the current state of the art in number theory assures us that computing the discrete logarithm for our numbers is hard.

We said above that the cryptographic community did not know of any practical solution to the key distribution problem until Diffie and Hellman published their paper. That is not entirely true. Malcolm John Williamson, a British mathematician and cryptographer, had discovered what we now call the Diffie-Hellman key exchange two years before them, in 1974. Williamson was working at the Government Communications Headquarters, the UK intelligence and communications agency, and therefore was not able to publish his discovery. It was made known many years later, in 1997.

ElGamal Encryption

Once we have the Diffie-Hellman key exchange, another possibility emerges. Two parties have agreed to a common, shared, secret key. Instead of using that key in a separate encryption method, we can take the key and use it directly to encrypt a message by performing a mathematical operation on the message. The requirements are that the result of the mathematical operation should not give any information on the message or key, and that the mathematical operation can be reversed, given the key. This idea lies behind the ElGamal encryption method, introduced by Taher Elgamal in 1984.[4]

The mathematical operation that we can use is surprisingly straightforward: we need just perform a modular multiplication, that is, multiplication followed by the modulo operator, of the message with the key. The result of the modular multiplication provides no information about the message or key. Then to decrypt the message, we need to undo the multiplication. If we did not use modular arithmetic, that would be a simple matter of dividing the ciphertext by the key. In modular arithmetic, things get more interesting.

Let's forget modular operations for a moment. If we multiply our message m with the shared secret s and get the ciphertext $c = m \cdot s$, we can recover the original message by dividing by s: $c / s = (m \cdot s) / s = m$. In ordinary, meaning nonmodular, arithmetic, for every integer $a \neq 0$, we can find a number b such that $a \cdot b = 1$; it is simply the reciprocal $b = 1 / a$. In our encryption scheme, the reciprocal of our secret is $1 / s$. We call b the *inverse* of a, and denote it by a^{-1}. Inverses are symmetric: when b is the inverse of a, a is the inverse of b. In modulo arithmetic, if a and b are inverses, it does not hold that $b = 1 / a$; in fact, both a and b are integers, and neither of them is a fraction. We call b the *modular multiplicative inverse* of a, but we also call it simply inverse for brevity. For example, if $a = 3$, then the modular multiplicative inverse of a modulo 40 is $b = 27$, because $3 \cdot 27 \bmod 40 = 81 \bmod 40 = 1$.

While in ordinary arithmetic we can always find the multiplicative inverse of a nonzero integer, that no longer holds in modular arithmetic. The modular multiplicative inverse of a number exists only if the greatest common

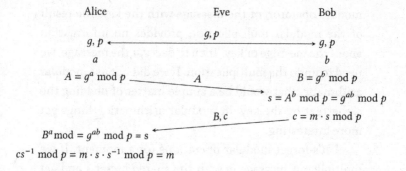

Figure 44

divisor of the number and the modulus is equal to one. When two numbers have a greatest common divisor equal to one, they are called *relatively prime* or *coprime*. Of course, if the modulus is itself prime, as it is in Diffie-Hellman, then the greatest common divisor of the number and modulus will be one, provided the number is not a multiple of the modulus. To find the modular multiplicative inverse, we can use a well-known algorithm called the *extended Euclidean algorithm*.

With that, we can now see the steps of ElGamal encryption and decryption, which are pretty similar to the familiar Diffie-Hellman key exchange (see figure 44):

1. Alice and Bob agree on a common number g, and they do that in public, with no secrecy involved. They also agree on a prime number that will be their common

modulus, which is not kept secret. We'll use p to denote the modulus.

2. Alice picks a number a that she keeps secret.

3. Alice mixes her secret number with the common number *taking the remainder with the modulus*. To do that, she raises the common number to the power of her secret number modulo p. We'll use A to denote Alice's result, so we have $A = g^a \bmod p$.

4. Alice sends A to Bob.

5. Bob picks a secret number b. He calculates $B = g^b \bmod p$ and $s = A^b \bmod p = g^{ab} \bmod p$. That's the Diffie-Hellman secret. Then he multiplies s with his secret message m to calculate $c = m \cdot s \bmod p$. He sends the pair (B, c) to Alice. This is the encryption step: the Diffie-Hellman key, when multiplied with the message, disguises it, and nobody can find the original message unless they can remove the disguise. That requires reversing the modular multiplication.

6. Given B and a, Alice can also calculate $s = B^a \bmod p$ $= g^{ab} \bmod p$, the Diffie-Hellman shared secret. Alice can decrypt Bob's message by finding the inverse of s, s^{-1}, and multiplying it with c to get the original message: $cs^{-1} \bmod p = m \cdot s \cdot s^{-1} \bmod p = m$. Alice is the sole person capable of reversing the multiplication of step 5 and revealing the message.

ElGamal is as secure as Diffie-Hellman, so we can be confident in using it. It is nice that the same construct can be used for more than one purpose. At the heart of the matter is the fact that for any $g^a \bmod p$ (Alice's A) and $g^b \bmod p$ (Bob's B), the value $g^{ab} \bmod p$ (the shared secret) is indistinguishable from any random value modulo p, so we cannot use $g^a \bmod p$ and $g^b \bmod p$ to break the system and find the shared secret. To be more accurate, this is an assumption, not a proven statement, and is called the *decisional Diffie-Hellman* (DDH) assumption. Mathematically, it is a stronger assumption than the assumption that we cannot solve the discrete logarithm problem. There are particular cases where the DDH does not hold, but the discrete logarithm assumption does. Beyond Diffie-Hellman and ElGamal, the DDH enables other efficient and strong cryptographic systems, to the point that Dan Boneh, a leading cryptographer, has likened it to a gold mine.[5]

RSA

Throughout our discussion on cryptography, we have been heeding a fundamental assumption that a message is encrypted to a ciphertext with a key and the ciphertext is decrypted to the original message using the same key. What if we drop that assumption? Could we devise a scheme where we could use *different keys* for encryption and decryption?

Could we devise a
scheme where we could
use different keys
for encryption and
decryption?

At first sight, this does not appear to make sense; after all, in our everyday experience, when we lock something with a key, we need the same key to unlock it. Dropping the assumption means that we would need a padlock with two different keys, so that if it is locked with one, it is unlocked with the other.

If Alice has such a padlock and pair of keys and wants to communicate securely with Bob, she will send the padlock and one of the two keys to Bob. Bob will get a box, put his message inside the box, close the padlock, and lock it with the key he got from Alice. When Alice gets the locked box back, she will use her other key to unlock the padlock and recover Bob's message, as shown in figure 45.

We want to do something similar in the digital realm. Suppose that we have a message, m, encoded as a number, that we want to encrypt. We would like to give Bob one key so that he can encrypt it and send the encrypted message to Alice. Then Alice would use the other key, which she has not divulged to anybody, to decrypt it. If we were able to do that, the key distribution problem would be solved because we would not distribute the decryption key at all. Alice would distribute freely one of the keys, keeping the other key secret, and secrecy would be guaranteed as long as she keeps the other key secure.

This idea forms the basis of *public key cryptography*. Instead of having one key as the foundation of encryption and decryption, public key cryptography posits that we

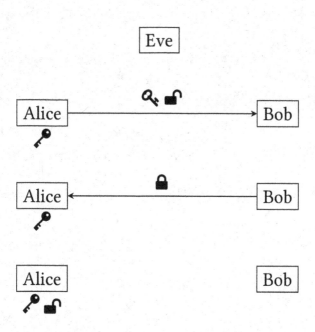

Figure 45

can have two keys: one for encryption, and one for decryption. We do not need to keep both keys secret. We make the encryption key public so that anybody who knows the public key can send us an encrypted message. But only the person who possesses the private key can decrypt it.

This is a major pivot in the way we think of cryptography: the encryption and decryption algorithms that we have seen up to now, from ancient times to today, use symmetric cryptography: the same key is used for

Instead of having one key as the foundation of encryption and decryption, public key cryptography posits that we can have two keys: one for encryption, and one for decryption.

both encryption and decryption. Public key cryptography breaks this assumption and ushers in asymmetric cryptography.

To get there, let us start with a simple operation. We find a large positive integer e, which we do not keep secret, and raise the message, m, to that power:

$$c = m^e$$

Now we need a way to get m back from c. That is trivial. If we have a value like $y = x^n$, and we want to get x from y, it is pretty straightforward—we'll take the nth root of y: $\sqrt[n]{y} = \sqrt[n]{x^n} = x$. For example, the square root of 4 is 2 ($\sqrt{4} = 2$), the cubic root of 8 is 2 ($\sqrt[3]{8} = \sqrt[3]{2^3} = 2$), the fourth root of 16 is 2 ($\sqrt[4]{16} = \sqrt[4]{2^4} = 2$). Instead of writing nth roots, we define the fractional power $y^{1/n}$ to be the nth root of y: $y^{1/n} = \sqrt[n]{y}$. This works nicely with the identity of raising a power to a power: $(x^y)^z = x^{yz}$, so $(x^y)^{1/y} = x^{y \cdot 1/y} = x^1 = x$.

Knowing this, if we create c as $c = m^e$, then we are able to find m immediately by taking the eth root of c, or, equivalently, raising c to $d = 1/e$:

$$c^d = (m^e)^d = m^{ed} = m^{e \cdot 1/e} = m$$

For example, suppose that $m = 2$ (to keep things simple). Then if we use $e = 5$, we have $c = 2^5 = 32$. If we now raise 32 to ⅕, we have $32^{1/5} = \sqrt[5]{32} = 2$.

Our scheme does not amount to much because Eve can intercept c and also immediately take the eth root of the ciphertext to recover the plaintext.

But now we add a twist. Rather than simply raising the plaintext to a power, we will raise it to a power and take the remainder modulo a chosen number n (no relation with the discussion of the nth root above).[6] That is, we will perform modular exponentiation so that we will have:

$c = m^e \bmod n$

This looks like Diffie-Hellman on the surface, but it isn't. In Diffie-Hellman, the exponents are secrets; this time, our secret, m, is the *base* of the exponentiation.

To get m back from c, we need to get the eth root of c modulo n. That is the crux. Getting the eth root of c modulo n is not easy. There is no such thing as $\sqrt[e]{c} \bmod n$. What we need to do is find a number d such that:

$m = c^d \bmod n$

The problem is that, when we are working with modular arithmetic, the number d is not simply the multiplicative inverse of e; it does not work to set $d = 1 / e$ and plug it into the above equation.

It seems that we are getting somewhere. We encrypt our message m as $c = m^e \bmod n$. We would like to decrypt the ciphertext c using $m = c^d \bmod n$, for some d, if only we knew how to find it.

In 1978, three researchers, Ron Rivest, Adi Shamir, and Leonard Adleman, described a way to do that, thus creating the RSA cryptosystem (after the first letter in each of their last names).[7] Although we cannot find d given any e, they found a way to generate e, d, and n *together*. In effect, the RSA cryptosystem describes how we can find three numbers, e, d, and n, such that whenever we perform an exponentiation modulo n of a message with *one of them*, we can recover the message by performing an exponentiation modulo n of the ciphertext with the *other number of the pair*.

Let's return to our usual cast of characters. Alice uses RSA to find three numbers e, d, and n, with the required property:

$$c = m^e \bmod n, \qquad m = c^d \bmod n$$

Alice will keep d a secret and not reveal it to anybody. As for e, she will make it public, along with n. She can put it into her online profile, website, email signature, or wherever. She can share the tuple (e, n) to the world; the tuple is her *public key*. She keeps d a secret; the tuple (d, n) is her *secret (private) key*. The two keys form a *key pair*, called a *public-private key pair*.

Bob gets the tuple (e, n). Bob uses the tuple to encrypt his message, calculating $c = m^e \bmod n$, and sends the

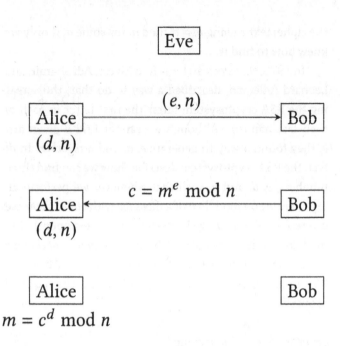

Figure 46

resulting c to Alice. Alice uses her tuple (d, n) to decrypt it, getting $m = c^d \bmod n$, as depicted in figure 46.

Eve intercepts c as well as (e, n). To decrypt the message, however, she needs to find d, and Alice has kept d a secret. So even though Eve can follow all the communication between Alice and Bob, she cannot decrypt the ciphertext. She could be tempted to find m by calculating the eth root of c modulo n, but (as you've probably guessed) there is no efficient way of doing that.

We can see RSA in action with a small example. Alice has generated her public-private key pair as $(e, n) = (17, 2773)$ and $(d, n) = (157, 2773)$. Bob wants to encrypt the number 920 and send it to Alice. He will ask Alice for $(e, n) = (17, 2773)$ and perform the calculation:

$c = 920^{17} \bmod 2773 = 948$

Then Bob will send $c = 948$ to Alice, and Alice will calculate:

$m = 948^{157} \bmod 2773 = 920$

So Alice will get the plaintext back correctly. The calculations may seem complicated, but not to a computer.

The example shows that the numbers e and d are not connected in an obvious way: with $e = 157$, to find the 157th modular root of a number $c = m^{157} \bmod 2773$, we have to raise the number c to $d = 17$ and take the remainder modulo $n = 2773$. And even if we know e, n, and $m^e \bmod n$, we cannot find d to carry out the operation.

The insight behind RSA is how to find the numbers e, d, and n in the first place. This is how:

1. Pick two distinct prime numbers, p and q.

2. The number n will be their product: $n = p \cdot q$.

3. Calculate the product $(p - 1) \cdot (q - 1)$. Pick a large integer, which will be e, such that there is no number (apart from 1) that divides both e and $(p - 1) \cdot (q - 1)$. To put it in more mathematical terms, their greatest common divisor is 1 and they are coprime.

4. Find the integer d such that the product $e \cdot d$ has the remainder 1 when divided by $(p - 1) \cdot (q - 1)$. That is, find the number d such that $e \cdot d \bmod (p - 1)(q - 1) = 1$.

In step 4, we have two numbers, e and d, such that their product is 1 modulo $(p - 1)(q - 1)$. In the modulo realm, then, e and d are inverses of each other. We meet again the modular multiplicative inverse that we introduced when we described ElGamal. In step 3, we find a large number e that is coprime to $(p - 1)(q - 1)$. We do that because then we know that e will have a multiplicative inverse modulo $(p - 1)(q - 1)$. One way to do that is to pick random numbers until we find one that is coprime. Then we know that the e we find in step 3 has a modular multiplicative inverse, which we'll find in step 4. In that step, we find e's inverse d using the extended Euclidean algorithm.

The security of RSA rests on the difficulty of finding d if we know only e and n, the public key. This ensures that it is not possible to find the private key from the public key. Once more, it is mathematics that tells us that, to the best of our knowledge, this is difficult. From the way e, d, and n are constructed, the number n is the product of two prime numbers, p and q, which we pick at random when we create our public and private keys. These two numbers we have to keep secret. That means that we have $n = p \cdot q$, but nobody else knows that. Eve, and anybody else, only knows n. If, having n, they could find the two prime numbers p and q, then they could run step 4 above, construct the secret d, and break RSA.

The *fundamental theorem of arithmetic* tells us that any integer greater than 1 can be written as a unique product of prime numbers, which are called its *prime factors*. The two numbers p and q are the prime factors of n. The process of breaking up a number to its prime factors is called *factorization*. Although every integer can be factored to primes, we do not know of an efficient algorithm to do so. Given n, we do not know how to find p and q efficiently. We can try different values for p and q, but if n is large (and we can make it enormous), applying such a brute-force approach will not work.

As in Diffie-Hellman and the discrete logarithm problem, there is no proof that an efficient algorithm for *integer prime factorization*, as the problem is formally called, does not exist. But we have not found any, and with the current state of knowledge in mathematics we believe it is unlikely that we will ever find such an algorithm.

Enough with mathematics. Getting back to an example of using RSA, suppose that Bob wants to encrypt the following phrase and send it to Alice:[8]

As we saw, Alice's public key is $(e, n) = (17, 2773)$. RSA performs all calculations modulo n, here 2773, so the message must be encoded in numbers less than 2773. In general, when we have calculations modulo n, all numbers will be from 0 up to $n - 1$, as these are the possible remainders of divisions by n. Therefore, in RSA we must ensure our message fits the modulo n; the same applies, for the same reason, in ElGamal encryption. In our example, we can do that by using a two-digit number per letter, including blank spaces; a blank will be 00, A will be 01, B will be 02, up to Z, which will be 26. In this encoding, two characters form a block that fits in 2773, so the message would be encoded as:

```
0920 0023 0119 0007 1805 0511 0020
1500 1305
```

In the above, 0920 is a block encoding I (09) and T (20); 0023 is a block encoding the blank (00) and W (23), and it goes like this for the rest of the message. Bob can take each block, encrypt it using Alice's public key, and send it to Alice. We already saw that the number 920 encrypts to 948. This is the encryption of the whole plaintext:

```
0948 1581 2243 1698 2423 0680 2624
2417 0813
```

Alice will take each block and decrypt it: 948 decrypts to 920, which decodes to *IT*, 1581 decrypts to 0023, which decodes to a space and *W*, 2243 decodes to 0018, which decodes to *AS*, and so forth along the rest.

At this point we have a method, RSA, that we can use to encrypt messages without suffering from the key distribution problem. An obvious question arises then: Why bother with AES and Diffie-Hellman at all? Doesn't RSA solve all of our cryptographic problems? Why would anybody want to use AES, which requires that we exchange keys using Diffie-Hellman? Surely it is way simpler to do everything with RSA?

The answer is that yes, it is simpler to use RSA instead of a combination of methods, yet in practice we rarely ever use RSA to encrypt messages. The reason is that RSA is *much* slower than a symmetric encryption cipher like AES. Depending on the implementation, RSA can be hundreds or thousands of times slower. That is counterintuitive given that AES involves the complex sequence of steps that we saw in the previous chapter while RSA uses only modular exponentiations. Yet the AES internals are much more computer friendly than RSA, and the sizes of the numbers involved are at a different scale. AES works with keys of 128, 192, or 256 bits while RSA needs keys that are thousands of bits long.

For that reason, RSA is really used as a key exchange mechanism, as an alternative to Diffie-Hellman. Bob encrypts a key using RSA and sends the key to Alice. Then Alice can use that key with AES or any other symmetric encryption algorithm. This combination of symmetric and asymmetric encryption is called *hybrid encryption* and is very common; ElGamal is also commonly used in hybrid encryption to encrypt a symmetric key.

What we have described here is the so-called textbook RSA or schoolbook RSA. This should alert you because when something is portrayed as textbook or schoolbook, it usually means that it is an ideal, which is seldom or ever used in practice. So it is with RSA: the textbook RSA should never be used in practice because it is insecure, having important vulnerabilities.

One vulnerability is that textbook RSA is deterministic. Like AES, for a particular key, the same plaintext will always be encrypted to the same ciphertext. That is a problem (remember Felix the Cat?) because an attacker may be able to deduce some information on the meaning of ciphertexts even without decrypting them. For instance, Bob may be sending to Alice a sequence of messages, some of them identical, like instructions to perform some action. If Eve intercepts the ciphertexts and observes the actions that Alice performs, she will be able to associate particular ciphertexts with actions. So Eve will know what the ciphertexts mean even without having revealed the underlying plaintexts.

Another vulnerability is that textbook RSA is *malleable*. A cryptographic method is malleable when an attacker can transform the ciphertext into another ciphertext that decrypts to a plaintext related to the original one. Therefore it is not secure under a chosen ciphertext attack, which we introduced in the previous chapter. In RSA, if Bob has created the ciphertext $c = m^e \bmod n$, then an adversary can create a new ciphertext $c' = t^e c \bmod n$ and send it to Alice. She will decrypt it with $(t^e c)^d \bmod n = t^{ed} m^{ed} \bmod n = t \cdot m \bmod n$. If the original message contained an agreed-on sum, the message from the decryption of c' will be t times modulo m the original sum—not an ideal state of affairs. To be fair, not just RSA but ElGamal also suffers from malleability, yet there are other schemes related to ElGamal that are nonmalleable.[9]

These two problems can be remedied in RSA by *padding*. We take the plaintext and some random data and combine these two before encryption. A scheme that uses RSA with padding is *optimal asymmetric encryption padding* (OAEP), or RSA-OAEP. This has been formalized as a standard, *PKCS #1* (Public Key Cryptography Standard #1), the first in a series of standards published by RSA Laboratories, a security company founded by the inventors of RSA.[10] Such standards are instrumental in taking a textbook description of a cryptographic method and making it suitable for use in the real world.

This leads to a warning for the reader: none of the modern cryptographic techniques we describe are meant to be used simply as presented here. It may seem that we are bashing RSA, but a similar caution applies to Diffie-Hellman, which in practice can be less secure than widely believed.[11] In the beginning of the book, we proclaimed that we aim to show how cryptography actually works. In the last couple of chapters, we do that by describing the fundamental concepts and the logic behind different methods. A cryptographic method, however, is a depiction of an algorithm. An architectural blueprint, even if accurate, is not a finished building. A lot of additional work and engineering decisions are required, taking into account the facts on the ground. Similarly, to turn cryptographic methods into actual products that can stand their ground against real adversaries, we must take care of many implementation details and guard against possible attacks that span the whole spectrum of activities required to go from a blueprint to a tangible artifact. This is an ongoing process, as possible weaknesses and vulnerabilities can be discovered long after the method is initially proposed. Still, remaining faithful to how something really works does not require going into every detail of its implementation. To understand how a tool is made, you must start by studying its design documents and diagrams; you do not need to know the manufacturing details—unless, that is, you are the manufacturer.

When we decide to use a cryptographic method, we should be careful to use a product that follows the relevant standards and has a good security track record. A good idea is to use *open-source* products—that is, products built with software whose source code is published and made available to the public so that anybody can inspect as well as study it for any possible vulnerabilities. We cautioned against security by obscurity in the previous chapter; transparency works best throughout the cryptographic spectrum of methods.

RSA completed the revolution that Diffie-Hellman started, as it was the first time that public key cryptography was disseminated to the cryptographic community. In an eerie parallel to the history of Diffie-Hellman, though, public key cryptography was known before to a select few. Clifford Cocks, working at the Government Communications Headquarters, had discovered an equivalent system back in 1973 but, like his colleague Malcolm John Williamson who had discovered Diffie-Hellman, his results remained a secret until they were declassified in 1997.

Digital Signatures

"On the Internet, nobody knows you're a dog," goes the caption of a cartoon that was published in the *New Yorker* on July 5, 1993. The cartoon, by Peter Steiner, features two dogs. One of them, sitting on a chair in front of a computer, speaks the caption to the second dog, who is sitting on the floor.

Although it is not so easy to hide our identity in the online world, the cartoon alludes to a real problem. If you receive a message from somebody, how do you know that the message is really from the alleged sender? You are probably safe to assume that it has not been sent by a dog, but while in the real world you rely on clues such as a signature to know that indeed the message has been written by its purported author, how can you link a digital message to its author? How can you prevent the author of the message repudiating that they have written it? A digital message can be copied an infinite amount of times, and every copy is as good as the original. Moreover, a digital message can be changed, and there won't be any smudges on it to indicate that there is something out of order.

To ensure authenticity, we take a leaf out of the physical world's book and transfer it to the digital one. As we noted, in the physical world we verify the author of a document by checking for their signature on it. We do the same in the digital world; the way we do it is with *digital signatures*, and digital signatures are possible with asymmetric encryption schemes like RSA.

Recall that the basic idea is that what we encrypt with one of the two keys in the public-private key pair can only be decrypted with the other key in the pair. Bob encrypts with Alice's public key, and Alice decrypts with her private key. But now we can interchange the order of exponentiation in RSA and still get a valid identity:

$$(m^d)^e \bmod n = m$$

Notice that we have swapped the positions of e and d in the original identity. According to mathematics, we can do that, and it is correct. But this is not just about fiddling with the exponents; the new identity has a real import in that it shows us that we can use the secret key d for encryption and the public key e for decryption.

Why should anybody want to do that? It means that we have Alice encrypt a message with her *private* key. The message is no longer secret because anybody with her public key (that is, everybody who cares, as the key is public) can decrypt it. But the public and private keys form an indissoluble pair. What is bound by one of the two keys can only be unbound by the other. Therefore when Bob uses Alice's public key to decrypt her message, he can be sure that it was encrypted with her private key. As long as Alice keeps her private key secret, Bob can be sure that the message was created by Alice and nobody else. In this way, Alice has *signed* her message. Everybody can decrypt Alice's message and, by doing so, everybody can be sure that this was indeed Alice's and nobody else's message. Alice no longer sends an unbreakable encryption of her message

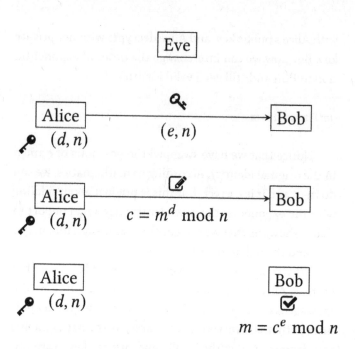

Figure 47

but rather her signature on the message, as shown in figure 47.

This exchange suffices to prove to Bob that the message comes from Alice, as long as he knows that it is Alice who has sent him her public key in the first place. He might know it because he got it directly from her. In general, however, knowing that Alice's public key does indeed come from Alice is a problem (think of the dog again). We solve the problem by using *digital certificates*; these are digital files that are digitally signed by authorities that we have agreed to trust and who attest that Alice's public key is indeed Alice's public key. It is analogous to what happens in the physical world; for instance, your passport is valid because it is issued by some public authority. A public key is valid because it has been certified by a public authority. What constitutes a public authority on the internet is different from what constitutes an authority offline, but the basic concept is the same. In the next chapter, we will see that digital certificates play an important role in internet communications.

There is a slight hitch in the scheme we have described, and it has to do with the fact that RSA can only operate on messages whose size does not exceed the modulo n. We can try to break up the message into chunks, as we described before, but that is insecure. Imagine that instead of signing a whole document, you cut it up into words and sign each one of them separately. Then somebody could take your individually signed words and stitch them together to create any signed message of their choosing. To get around the problem, we use *digital fingerprints*. A fingerprint uniquely identifies a person, but is considerably smaller and easier to carry around than the person itself. A digital fingerprint, also called a *message digest*, is something similar. It is something that we derive from a digital document and uniquely identifies that document. The way this works is with special algorithms that read the whole document and perform some speedy calculations on its contents. The end result is a tiny piece of data, for example 8 bytes (256 bits) long, that we are confident would only come out of that particular document. These algorithms are called *hash algorithms* (you can think that they make a hash of the contents of the document) and implemented in *hash functions*.

Hash algorithms are an important element of cryptography on their own; we'll see that they are an integral part of cryptographic protocols and applications. Let's consider what a hash algorithm really achieves. It takes an input, which can be considerably large. Based on this input, it computes a small output, of a fixed size, such as 256 bits. As we want that output to operate as a digital fingerprint of the input, it must be unique. Some thought will show that it is not possible to guarantee that this will always happen. If our documents are 10 kilobytes long (tiny documents by today's standards), each one of them is $10{,}000 \times 8 = 80{,}000$ bits long. There are $2^{80{,}000}$ possible documents of 10 kilobytes (why? because each of the 80,000 bits can take two values). If our hash values are 256 bits long, we have only 2^{256} unique fingerprints for $2^{80{,}000}$ possible documents. True, these powers of 2 are preposterously large; be that as it may, many documents will hash to the same value. When two documents hash to the same value, we say we have a *collision*.

Even though it is theoretically impossible to avoid collisions altogether, good hash functions have the property that collisions are extremely unlikely—after all, we are never going to hash anywhere near $2^{80,000}$ documents. Moreover, their output looks random and does not give any cue as to their input; it is not possible to recover any information about the original document from its hash. That means that it is not possible to go back to the original document itself if we have only its hash value. A hash algorithm is then a one-way function. Cryptographers over the years have developed hash functions that meet the above properties. A set of hash functions that is commonly used in cryptography is the SHA-2 (secure hash algorithm 2) family, designed by the NSA and published in 2001. The different members of the SHA-2 family produce hash values of different sizes. A popular choice is the SHA-256 function, producing, as we would expect, 256 bit hashes.[12]

To see what a SHA-256 fingerprint means, take the full text of James Joyce's *Ulysses*, which runs to 1,520,795 bytes or 12,166,360 bits. The SHA-256 digest of the text is the string:

```
9ce5a3ee947c7a66c0967fc719e468d44d5efa
fd8d23488f57d4cd7181ae7289
```

This string uniquely identifies *Ulysses*, as it is extremely unlikely that we can find another document with the same SHA-256 value. The hash value bears no discernible relation to the original text. Indeed, the text begins with the title, "ULYSSES." If we change the title to "uLYSSES," which corresponds to flipping a single bit to change the uppercase U (its binary representation in a computer is 1010101) to the lowercase u (its binary representation in a computer is 1110101), the new SHA-256 hash value is:

> 88a98f4d500906200c03772b41addc076f66bb
> ff8069f61fa2a1fd81be6218d1

A single bit flipped among more than 12 million; a completely different hash value.

Back to signing. When Alice wants to sign a document and send it to Bob, she does not really sign the document itself. She produces its digital fingerprint using a hash function that creates a fingerprint smaller than the modulus n and signs the fingerprint. She sends the signed fingerprint along with the document to Bob. Bob gets the message and its digital fingerprint. He knows that the fingerprint could only have been created by Alice because it was signed by her. So he simply runs the same fingerprint-generation algorithm on the message and checks that he gets exactly the same fingerprint as the one that came signed by Alice.

Hashing is an essential component of using RSA-based signatures in the real world. Textbook RSA signatures, like textbook RSA encryption, are only suitable for educational purposes. If Alice really wants to sign a message, she will not simply encrypt it with her private key. She will probably use a scheme like RSASSA-PSS (RSA signature scheme with appendix—probabilistic signature scheme), or simply RSA-PSS, which uses hashing and padding prior to the actual RSA signing. RSASSA-PSS is part of PKCS #1, which we encountered before.

Something that may not be immediately obvious is that digital signatures do not imply secrecy. The message and fingerprint are communicated as plaintext in the steps we described above. In fact, secrecy via encryption is completely orthogonal to digital signatures. If Alice and Bob want to communicate securely *and* have their messages signed, they can add encryption on top of the signing process. That means that Alice will not send the message and fingerprint as plaintext but rather as ciphertexts. To create the ciphertexts, she can use any method she wants. She can use Diffie-Hellman to exchange a key with Bob and then encrypt all communication with Bob (the message and RSA-signed fingerprint) with AES using the key they exchanged. Or she can use RSA to exchange a key with Bob and then use AES to send the message along with the RSA-signed fingerprint to Bob. The second scenario showcases the versatility of asymmetric encryption, which is used for different purposes in the same message exchange.

PROTOCOLS AND APPLICATIONS

We have seen the basic elements of cryptography: encryption and decryption, and how to exchange keys so that we can encrypt and decrypt securely. In our everyday lives, however, we are not likely to find ourselves exchanging keys, encrypting and decrypting, at least not visibly or consciously. We can communicate securely through the internet, so all of this must somehow happen, but it happens behind the scenes.

You can think of the basic elements of cryptography as building blocks, LEGO bricks if you will, that are combined to build the applications that we use. The way to combine the building blocks to deliver an application is through *protocols*. In real life, protocols are agreed on, often officially, and specify the rules to be followed in particular occasions. But they are not only pomp and circumstance. We use informal protocols in our everyday dealings. When making a phone call, the one who picks up the phone usually starts with a greeting, like "hi" or "hello"; this is the cue that the discussion can begin. The caller, if not already known, will then probably announce themselves. After the mutual introduction, the call will continue until the end is announced, such as with a "bye."

In cryptography, there are many different protocols for all the different things that we want to perform. In this chapter, we will sketch a few of them, which will hopefully allow you to appreciate the breadth of cryptographic applications beyond the basic encryption and decryption of messages.

We will start with how our communication is secured on the internet when we communicate with different websites. We must encrypt the data we exchange, but before that we want to agree on how exactly to encrypt the data. We also need to verify that the website we are interacting with is genuine. When you step into a branch of your bank, you know that it is an actual branch of your real bank— unless somebody has set up a fake bank office (this is arguably not easy for a full-fledged bank branch, but setting up a fake ATM is a more practical proposition). When you visit your bank's website, how do you know that it is the website of your actual bank and not some setup that will steal your e-banking credentials?

Going beyond solving communication problems between two parties, cryptography can be used for more advanced scenarios. One of them is how to share a secret between a number of people so that the secret can be revealed only when a minimum number of them agree to do so. Imagine you have a box that is locked with five keys, distributed to different key holders, and the keys are made in such a way that the box can be opened when, say, no less than three of the key holders come together and insert their keys in the lock. It may seem a bit like magic, but we'll see how to do that with cryptography.

From secret sharing, it is a short jump to see how different parties can compute something together, without any of the involved parties being able to see the whole picture and come to a result on which all of them agree. Imagine that two different government agencies hold financial information on the citizens of the country; we would like to somehow amalgamate the information from the two different sources without revealing the information from one agency to the other one. This is the subject of *secure multiparty computation* (MPC), and we'll see how cryptographic protocols enable us to do it.

Transport Layer Security

The transport layer security (TLS) protocol secures internet communications that take place with our browsers. It is an essential part of the digital infrastructure—any activity from entering a username and password to making financial transactions over the web would not be secure, and therefore possible, without TLS. That is because the internet was not designed to provide secure communications. The internet works with a suite of protocols called TCP/IP (for transport control protocol / internet protocol) that allows computers around the world to communicate by establishing virtual connections between them. The connections are virtual because there need not be a direct cable connecting the two computers that communicate. They communicate by exchanging data that travels in packets hopping on intermediaries called *routers*, which receive data packets and forward them toward their final destination, like an electronic postal service.

The internet was initially developed by the US Defense Advanced Research Projects Agency (DARPA) in the 1960s and 1970s, and its humble origins belie what it would become in just a couple of decades. Figure 48 shows the first internetworked connection between the United States, United Kingdom, and Norway, from a demonstration on November 22, 1977.[1]

There is little need for security when you know everybody who is connected on the network and are on friendly terms with them. To get an idea of this, note that one of the first transmissions in the evolution of the internet originated from a van in the parking lot of a beer garden, Rossotti's Alpine Inn, in Portola Valley, California. Cables

The internet was not designed to provide secure communications.

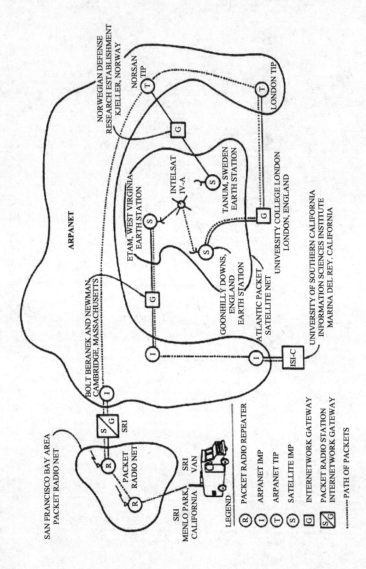

ARPANET

NORWEGIAN DEFENSE
RESEARCH ESTABLISHMENT
KJELLER, NORWAY

NORSAN
TIP

LONDON TIP

INTELSAT
IV-A

TANUM, SWEDEN
EARTH STATION

ETAM, WEST VIRGINIA
EARTH STATION

UNIVERSITY COLLEGE LONDON
LONDON, ENGLAND

BOLT BERANEK AND NEWMAN
CAMBRIDGE, MASSACHUSETTS

GOONHILLY DOWNS,
ENGLAND
EARTH STATION

ATLANTIC PACKET
SATELLITE NET

UNIVERSITY OF SOUTHERN CALIFORNIA
INFORMATION SCIENCES INSTITUTE
MARINA DEL REY, CALIFORNIA

ISI-C

SRI

SAN FRANCISCO BAY AREA
PACKET RADIO NET

PACKET
RADIO NET

SRI
MENLO PARK,
CALIFORNIA

SRI VAN

LEGEND

(R) PACKET RADIO REPEATER
(I) ARPANET IMP
(T) ARPANET TIP
(S) SATELLITE IMP
(G) INTERNETWORK GATEWAY
(S/G) PACKET RADIO STATION
INTERNETWORK GATEWAY
---------- PATH OF PACKETS

Figure 48

ran from the van to one of the picnic tables, where a report was typed and sent using TCP.

Unfortunately, digital communications is not all beer and skittles. The internet grew way beyond its initial community and thus security became a concern. The internet's guiding principles and TCP/IP, though, have largely remained the same. That stands as witness to the foresight of the people who invented them. It also means that the connections provided by TCP/IP must be secured by building protocols that operate on top of the TCP/IP suite.

That is indeed what has happened. With TCP/IP as the foundation of the internet, additional mechanisms have been developed that operate on top of the virtual connections offered by TCP/IP to remedy the absence of security guarantees. TLS is the result of a long evolution starting in the 1990s. It was preceded by the now-deprecated secure sockets layer (SSL) protocols versions 1.0, 2.0, and 3.0. TLS itself has gone through versions 1.0, 1.1, and 1.2. The current version as of this writing, 1.3, in various aspects prunes down and simplifies TLS 1.2.[2] Still, it is a complicated protocol, and we will only present an abridged version here. Even that will give us the opportunity to see how different cryptographic algorithms that we have described, for symmetric cryptography, key exchange, and public key cryptography, fit together to enable secure communication over the web.

When a browser communicates with a website, it usually asks the website for something—for example, to display a web page. In more technical terms, the browser issues a *request* and expects a *response* from the website. The browser plays the role of the *client*, and the computer responding on the website plays the role of the *server*. When we have described communications between humans, we were content with Alice and Bob. As we will now be dealing with communication between programs, we'll adopt the client-server naming convention.

When they begin their communication, or *TLS session* as it is called, the client and the server perform a series of steps called the *TLS handshake protocol*. The handshake protocol is responsible for the following:

• Data will be encrypted using a symmetric encryption algorithm. The client and the server must agree on the exact details of the encryption algorithm.

• The client and the server must agree on the shared secret key that they will use with the symmetric encryption algorithm.

• The client must be certain that it is communicating with the genuine server and not with any impostor.

Let us take the above in more detail to see how TLS achieves them. The client starts the interchange by sending a special message to the server called *ClientHello*. In ClientHello, the client spells out an ordered list of the *cipher suites* it supports. A cipher suite comprises the symmetric encryption algorithm and length of the symmetric key to be used, along with the mode. AES may operate under either the GCM or the CCM mode, and AES is not the sole algorithm that is supported by TLS. The list gives the client's preference on the algorithm to be used, with the highest precedence given first. The client also sends one or more parts of a key exchange algorithm in ClientHello that the client expects to be supported by the server. Recall the Diffie-Hellman key exchange, where Alice sends to Bob the information needed to create a shared key with Bob.

Once the server receives ClientHello, it responds with a *ServerHello* message. The ServerHello message specifies the encryption algorithm from the list sent in ClientHello that the server has chosen. It also includes the server's part for the key exchange based on the client's expectations.

The server now has at its disposal the information it needs in order to derive the symmetric key that will be used for encrypting data. It goes on to calculate the shared secret key. Once the client receives the ServerHello message, it also calculates the same secret key. Now that both parties have calculated the shared secret key, all communication will be encrypted using that key and the symmetric encryption algorithm they have agreed to use.

There is another issue that must be resolved before the communication between the client and server can begin in earnest. The client—that is, the browser—communicates with a server. The only thing the client knows about the server is its address, which the human user enters in the browser. For well-known entities like the White House, the user can be confident that the address www.whitehouse.gov really belongs to the residence and office at 1600 Pennsylvania Avenue NW, Washington, DC. In general, however, things may not be so obvious. When you type in a web address, how can you be sure that this web address belongs to the entity to which it purports to belong? You are a new customer at a bank and wish to avail yourself of its online services. You are given its web address. Are you absolutely certain that this web address belongs to that particular bank?

To solve the problem, TLS uses digital certificates. A digital certificate is an electronic attestation for something. There are various kinds of digital certificates. At a minimum, a certificate attests that a particular public key belongs to a particular web server, or *host* as it is called—because it hosts a website or service. The certificate itself is signed by an entity called a *certificate authority*. A certificate authority is like a public authority in the digital realm. It is a public or private organization that gives its imprimatur on the contents of the certificate.

After the agreement on the shared secret key and before the exchange of the actual data begins, the server signs, with its private key, a hash of the messages of the handshake protocol. The hash acts like a summary of the handshake (although unlike a summary, it is only digital data, not humanly readable). Then it sends its certificate, along with the signed hash, to the client. When the client receives them, it gets the server's public key from the certificate, along with the assurance, thanks to the certificate, that the public key really belongs to that server. Then it uses the server's public key to verify that the server has indeed signed the handshake summary. Following the verification, the client now knows that it has performed the handshake with the hostname's rightful owner.

Right now it is not unreasonable that you throw up your hands in despair at the number of keys that you see being used in TLS. Here is the lowdown so that we have everything in one place:

• The client and the server agree on a common shared key that will be used for encrypting the data during their communication using a symmetric encryption algorithm.

• To do that, they have to perform a key exchange like in Diffie-Hellman.

• The server must convince the client that the client is communicating with the authentic host. To do that, the server must sign the handshake messages with its private key and provide to the client the corresponding public key.

- The client gets the server's corresponding public key from the server's certificate. The client knows that the certificate is authentic because it is signed with the private key of a certificate authority.

- The client can verify the certificate authority's signature by using the certificate authority's public key.

There are two kinds of certificate authorities. A *root certificate authority* is trusted by the browser, and its public key is stored in the browser. An *intermediate certificate authority* is not directly trusted by the browser, but it has its public key signed by another certificate authority. That certificate authority can be a root certificate authority or another intermediate certificate authority whose public key must be signed by yet another certificate authority, and so on, forming a *chain of trust* until we reach a root certificate authority. Root certificate authorities are well-known entities vetted by the implementers of web browsers.

We mentioned that a server certificate at a minimum binds a hostname with a public key. There are different kinds of server certificates according to the attestations they offer. The simplest ones only establish the relationship between hostnames and keys. Other server certificates contain more attestations that prove not only the hostname but also the legal entity of the owner of the certificate. The kind of certificate used by a website depends on the kind of website and the intended audience. A banking website, for instance, will need a certificate with additional information such as its verified legal name and address.

Once the handshake protocol of TLS has finished, the transmission of the actual data can begin. This is governed by the *TLS record protocol*, which describes the format of TLS records—that is, packets that contain the encrypted data.

All of this happens with most websites we visit every day. The requests and responses exchanged between a client, like our web browser, and a server are specified by yet another protocol, the *hypertext transfer protocol*, or HTTP. When the HTTP communication is encrypted using TLS, we have the *hypertext transfer protocol secure* (HTTPS). We know when we are using HTTPS instead of plain HTTP by the *scheme* used in a *uniform resource locator* (URL) or web address: it is https instead of plain http. Web browsers also allow us to peek into the details of the HTTPS and TLS connection; they typically display a locked padlock icon near the URL we are visiting. By clicking on it, we can get the secure connection details. Furthermore, web browsers will warn us if something goes wrong, particularly with the server's certificate. Instead of displaying the web page we expect to see, we'll get an alarming warning against proceeding to visit the website, as its authenticity cannot be determined.

Secret Sharing

We have seen that the security of a cryptographic mechanism must reside solely in its key. We have described different mechanisms that can encrypt our data safely, either with a single, symmetric key, or with a pair of public and private keys.

In real life, we come on situations where a key must be shared among different people. It is likely that more than one person has a key to our house (either a physical key or a combination, depending on our lock). Similarly in the digital realm, we may need to share a key among a number of persons. A digital key being a sequence of bits, it is easy to copy and share it among as many people as we want.

But now consider a somewhat different scenario. We have a safe that we want to secure so that it can be opened not by a single person in knowledge of the combination but instead when a number of persons convene and enter their part of the combination in the lock. In effect, we want to share the key among a number of persons so that all of them are needed in order to open the safe.

But what if something happens to one of the key bearers? If they are no longer around, we may not be able to open the safe anymore. To avoid this, we can think of a scheme in which a number of persons are issued parts of the combination, but only a subset of them is needed in order to unlock the safe. We could have six key bearers, but if four of them entered the combinations, the lock would open.

This idea extends directly to cryptography. We want to be able to share a secret among a number of persons. Although each person has part of the secret, they are not able to reconstruct the whole secret. Only if the required number of participants come together and each of them provides their own part of the secret will the key be reconstructed. We may split the secret in six parts and require that at least four of them, no less, be brought together in order to reconstruct the secret. Moreover, a person by themselves will not be able to derive any information from the secret, despite the fact that they hold part of it. Even if some of the participants collude, if they are even a single participant short of the required threshold, they should not be able to learn anything about the secret.

In cryptography, this is an instance of *secret sharing*. One of the first secret-sharing schemes was developed by Adi Shamir of RSA fame (the *S* in the acronym).[3] We can describe how it works by starting with a geometric interpretation.

Let's start with a given number of points. Mathematical analysis tells us that there is an infinite number of particular kinds of curves that interpolate between a given set of points with a specific number of peaks and troughs. For example, if we have three points, there is an infinite

We want to be able to share a secret among a number of persons. Although each person has part of the secret, they are not able to reconstruct the whole secret.

number of such curves with one peak and one trough that pass through the three points; see the left side of figure 49. If we want to pinpoint exactly one of these infinite curves, we need one additional point—that is, four points in total; see the right side of figure 49.[4]

The figure shows how we can create a secret-sharing scheme. We want to share a secret among six people so that at least four of them must cooperate in order to get the whole secret. Our secret will be a number. We will pick one curve that cuts the vertical axis on that secret number. As an example, say our secret is the number 896 and the corresponding curve is the one curve we have identified on the right of figure 49. From that curve, we pick six points that we distribute among our secret bearers. In order to find the secret number, the secret bearers must reconstruct the curve. Any fewer than four have no way to reconstruct the curve, as there are infinite curves passing through three points or fewer, as we see on the left of figure 49. But if four or more do share their points, as happens on the right-hand side of the figure, they can reconstruct the initial curve. They can then find its intersection with the vertical axis, 896, which is the secret.

In reality, we do not go about drawing curves. Let us tread lightly for a bit on mathematical analysis. A curve like the ones we have been drawing is a *polynomial*. A polynomial is a mathematical expression that is built from a sum of *terms*, where each term is the product of variables,

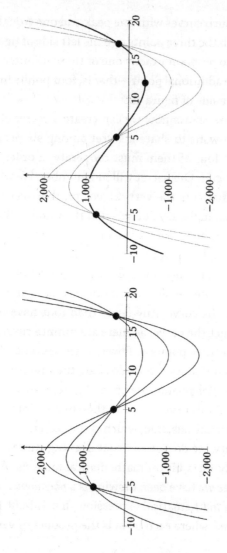

Figure 49

each of which can be raised to integer powers, and a constant number, called a *coefficient*. Here we will be using polynomials with only one variable, x. Geometrically, a polynomial that contains only the first power of x, like $3x + 5$, describes a straight line. A polynomial that contains a higher power of x, like $2x^2 + 3$, describes a curve. The highest power of x in the polynomial determines the *degree* of the polynomial. So $3x + 5$ is a first-degree polynomial, while $2x^2 - 5y + 3$ is a second-degree polynomial. A polynomial having degree n will cut the horizontal axis in up to n points, and will have up to $n - 1$ peaks and troughs—that is, inflection points. The curve in figure 49 corresponds to the polynomial $x^3 - 15x^2 - 72x + 896$, a third-degree polynomial. Note that 896 is a term with 896 being the constant and the variable x raised to the zeroth power $896 = 896x^0$, consistent with our definition. We call the term with the zeroth power the *zeroth term* of the polynomial.

There is an infinite number of polynomials of degree n passing through n given points, but there is only one polynomial of degree n passing through $n + 1$ points. Given this, in order to share a key among n people so that at least k must contribute their secret share to recover the whole secret, we can work as follows:

1. Create a polynomial of degree $k - 1$ that passes from the point with coordinates $(0, s)$, where s is our secret. All that is needed to pass through $(0, s)$ is to have s as the

zeroth term of the polynomial, as we did with 896 in our example. The other coefficients of the polynomial can be picked at random (and should not be revealed).

2. We select n distinct points from the polynomial; that is, we evaluate it for n different values of x. The value of the polynomial for each x is the y coordinate of a point. We distribute the points to the participants of the protocol.

3. If k or more participants pool their shares, they can reconstruct the original polynomial using a method called *Lagrangian interpolation*.

4. The participants evaluate the polynomial for $x = 0$ and recover the secret s.

The scheme will work in theory, but there is a problem in practice. Although there are infinite polynomials passing through $k - 1$ points, Eve, a malicious participant in the protocol, can exploit the fact that polynomials are, in a way, well-behaved curves, with their smooth peaks and troughs. Knowing that, and with some algebraic manipulations, she can considerably narrow down the range of possible curves. Instead of having to guess a secret among an infinite number of curves, she can try to guess it from only a limited amount of possibilities.

The solution to the problem is something we have seen before in our discussion of the Diffie-Hellman key

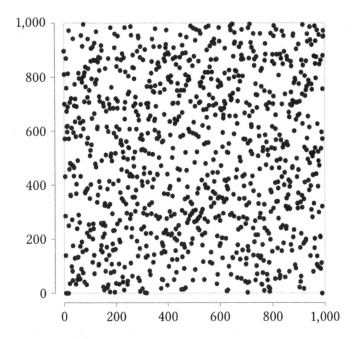

Figure 50

exchange. Rather than working with polynomials, we work with polynomials modulo a prime number. For example, instead of working with the polynomial $x^3 - 15x^2 - 72x + 896$, we work with the polynomial $x^3 - 15x^2 - 72x + 896 \mod 997$. This wreaks havoc on the predictability of curves that pass through the given points. Figure 50 shows the values of the polynomial for the natural numbers 0 through 997. From a gracile, sinuous curve, we get a haphazard scatter—which is want we want in order to thwart Eve's chances of guessing our secret.

Secure MPC

In the early 2010s, alarm bells went off in Estonia, a country with advanced e-government services as well as information and communication technology (ICT) awareness. The problem was that 43 percent of the students who had enrolled in ICT degrees in the years 2006 to 2012 had quit their studies by December 2012. Two competing hypotheses were put forward to explain the high dropout rate: First, that students were hired by companies even in their first year in the university, and it was possible that such students did not see an advantage in finishing their degree. Second, that the high dropout rate might be attributed to the increase in students enrolling in ICT courses and then finding the subject too hard.

The problem could be resolved by combining data from two different sources. The Ministry of Education had the records on higher education. The Ministry of Finance had the data on tax records. The two sets of data taken together could indicate which students were working, allowing an investigation into the link between getting hired and dropping out. The Estonian government, however, like other governments where data protection laws are in place, could not pool information from the two different sources. Data sharing between the Ministries of Education and Finance was not allowed under the existing legislation.

Moving to the United States, in 2016 the Boston Women's Workforce Council wanted to investigate issues impacting women in the workplace, one of them being the gender wage gap. Companies could anonymously report data broken down by gender, ethnicity, and level of employment. Yet those companies may have been unwilling to share such information; furthermore, the entity collecting the data for the analysis needed to be trusted by all and bore the onus of ensuring that no sensitive data was exposed.

Let's move again. In the private sector, companies that advertise online want to know the rate of *advertising conversion*—that is, the rate of people who see an advertisement and actually click on the ad (and then hopefully buy the advertised product). The problem is that when the customer does not buy the product online but instead buys it in the company's brick-and-mortar store, it is not possible to track the connection between the advertisement and purchase. The data needed to make that connection is split between two parts: the ad supplier, who knows which users have seen which ads, and the seller, who knows who has actually made a purchase. At the same time, the two parties are unwilling to share their data, but both of them would like to compute how many users saw an ad and then made a purchase, and the total amount the users spent.

The three problems above have been solved by secure multiparty computation, a field of cryptography studying methods that allow a set of parties to make computations on their data while keeping their data private. MPC has been studied for over three decades, but it is in the last decade that progress has been made to push MPC to practical applications.[5]

In Estonia, tax and higher education records were collected in an encrypted format, and then the analysis was carried out on the encrypted data, without decrypting it. The analysis showed that undergraduate ICT students do not work more than non-ICT students, and most of the bachelor's ICT students do not work in the ICT sector. In Boston, contributors could submit their data privately to a service provider that could not observe any of the individual inputs. The service provider analyzed the submitted data without impinging on the privacy of the submissions and reported the aggregate results. The data represented 166,705 employees across 114 companies, or about 16 percent of the Greater Boston area workforce. The gender wage gap was found to be even larger than what had been estimated by the US Bureau of Labor Statistics. As for the advertising conversion problem, Google has solved it by using a protocol for computing the intersection of two sets in a privacy-preserving manner.[6]

An MPC application can combine different cryptographic techniques and protocols. A common component of MPC applications is a secret-sharing scheme like Shamir secret sharing. An important technique is *homomorphic encryption*, in which computations can be performed directly on encrypted data without first decrypting it. We have already seen homomorphic encryption, even though we did not know it. In RSA, the product of two ciphertexts is equal to the encryption of the product of the corresponding plaintexts. So we do not need to decrypt the two ciphertexts before multiplying them. This follows from the properties of modular arithmetic linking two ciphertexts, c_1, c_2, and their plaintexts, m_1, m_2:

$$c_1 c_2 = (m_1^e \bmod n)(m_2^e \bmod n) = (m_1 m_2)^e \bmod n$$

The term on the left is the product of the encryptions; the term on the right is the encryption of the product of the plaintexts m_1, m_2.

Unfortunately, most MPC protocols are too complicated for us to present them here. But we can gain an idea of how MPC can work with a couple of simple examples. For the first one, we start with two parties, each of which has a set of data. The two parties wish to find the intersection of the two sets—that is, which elements exist in both sets—without revealing the full contents of their sets to each other or anybody else. That is called the *private set intersection* problem. The problem underlies the ad conversion application, but it is far more general. It arises, for instance, in DNA testing, where we want to find commonalities between genomes without revealing the full genomes.

A simple way to solve the problem is for each of the two parties, Alice and Bob, to use the same hash function on each of the elements of their own dataset. They can use the SHA-256 function that we encountered when discussing digital signatures. They must also decide on a random number that they will use as an input to SHA-256 in addition to each element they want to hash. In cryptography, we call random data that is added as additional input to a one-way hash function *salt*. The salt guarantees that the output of the hash function will be different each time the same data is hashed with a different salt.

Suppose that Alice and Bob want to compare song lists; they want to know which songs they have in common, but they do not want to reveal any of the songs. If we denote the salt with s and each of Alice's song tracks with $a_1, a_2, \ldots, a_n$, then Alice sends to Bob the hashed values SHA-256(s, a_1), SHA-256(s, a_2), $\ldots$, SHA-256(s, a_n). Bob does the same on his side, hashing his song tracks $b_1, b_2, \ldots, b_m$ and sending to Alice the hashed values SHA-256(s, b_1), SHA-256(s, b_2), $\ldots$, SHA-256(s, b_m).

Alice and Bob compare what they have received with what they have sent. They know that any tracks i and j that they find with SHA-256(s, a_i) = SHA-256(s, b_j) refer to the same song. They have recorded which song corresponds to which hash value they produced, so they can go back and identify each song they have in common. As for the rest of the songs, they are none the wiser, as they cannot reverse the hashed value to the originating track—remember, a hash function is one-way only.

The protocol is privacy preserving not only with respect to Alice and Bob but also against any eavesdropper, like Eve, who intercepts the hashed values produced by the two protocol participants. If Eve has a vast song catalog, she could try to hash all of her songs and find matches with Alice and Bob's hashed songs. That's where the salt enters the picture: as long as Eve does not know the salt, she cannot produce the target hash values, even if she is in possession of the same original data (here, songs) to be hashed.[7]

For a second MPC protocol example, suppose that we have again Alice and Bob, each one of them in possession of a secret number: Alice has x_1, and Bob has x_2. They want to find the product of their secrets without revealing their secrets to each other or anybody else. To do that, they will call on their friend Charlie and proceed as follows:[8]

1. Alice generates a random number a. She sends a to Charlie and $a + x_1$ to Bob.

2. Bobs generates a random number b. He sends b to Charlie and $b + x_2$ to Alice.

3. Alice calculates her share of the product $s_A = -a(b + x_2)$.
   Bob calculates his share of the product $s_B = x_2(a + x_1)$.
   Charlie calculates his share of the product $s_C = ab$.

4. Alice, Bob, and Charlie pool their shares s_A, s_B, and s_C.
   You can verify that $s_A + s_B + s_C = x_1 x_2$. The sum of their
shares is the product of Alice and Bob's secrets.

Neither Alice, Bob, nor Charlie can calculate the product
without the input of the other two parties. And none of
them can learn anything apart from the values they receive from each other. They cannot uncover Alice and
Bob's secret factors of the product.

Apart from protocols such as the above, which enable
MPC for a particular application, researchers have developed *general MPC protocols*—that is, protocols that can
be used to compute any function. The idea is to represent
the function that we want to compute in a special form,
called a *circuit*. Typically a circuit comprises simple components, such as simple logical operations, called *gates*.
For instance, the AND gate takes two inputs that may be
true or false and outputs true when both of the inputs are
true. The OR gate takes two inputs that may be true or
false and outputs true when either of them is true. And we
have our familiar XOR, a gate that takes two inputs that
may be true or false and outputs true when exactly one of
them is true. The representation is called a circuit precisely

because these are the components that are used to build electronic circuits.

In a typical setting, Alice and Bob want to calculate a function that requires input from both of them. They want to get the result of the function, but they do not want to reveal to each other their inputs. Here is how they can do it:

1. Alice starts with a circuit representing the function they want to calculate.

2. Alice encrypts the circuit using a procedure called *garbling*. She gives the encrypted, garbled circuit to Bob, along with her input encrypted in a way that can be understood by the garbled circuit.

3. Bob needs to encrypt his own input in a way compatible with Alice's encryption so that it is also understood by the garbled circuit. That means he needs Alice to encrypt his input without Alice getting to know Bob's input. He can achieve that using a cryptographic technique called *oblivious transfer*.

4. Having obtained the encryption of his input, Bob can now run—that is, evaluate—the garbled circuit with both Alice's and his own encrypted inputs and get the output of the garbled circuit. From that, Alice and Bob can get the output of the original circuit.

It is worth dwelling for a moment on oblivious transfer because it is remarkable in itself. Bob's input is a sequence of bits. He wants Alice to encrypt each one of them for him without actually revealing them to Alice. Alice has two encrypted messages, c_0 and c_1, corresponding to the encryption of 0 and 1, respectively. Bob uses a technique called "1–2 oblivious transfer" or "1 out of 2 oblivious transfer," based on asymmetric encryption like RSA. With 1–2 oblivious transfer, Bob can get Alice to give him c_0 or c_1, depending on the value of his own bit, with Alice remaining oblivious to the value of Bob's bit.[9]

A SAUCERFUL OF SECRETS

A fascinating and challenging part of cryptography is that it is a vibrant, fast-evolving field. Many of the hot topics of cryptography today did not even exist when this author was a student in the 1990s. It would be negligent for an introduction to cryptography, such as this one, not to touch on some of the remarkable discoveries and inventions that have occurred in the last few decades.

At the same time, it is not remotely possible to cover all the modern developments in cryptography. In this chapter, we will present a select few of these developments that are a big part of the conversation in today's cryptography.

We have seen that modern cryptography has a strong mathematical foundation. We are fiddling with numbers to encrypt and decrypt our messages. But what if we expand our scope? In mathematics, operations are not restricted to our familiar numbers. We can define mathematical

This leads us to elliptic curve cryptography, where we can define operations like addition and multiplication on things like points on a plane instead of numbers.

operations in other constructs. This leads us to elliptic curve cryptography (ECC), where we can define operations like addition and multiplication on things like points on a plane instead of numbers. Elliptic curves, a strange beast to begin with, are elegant; we can approach them without diving into higher mathematics, and they are well worth the effort to appreciate them. That is important because ECC allows us to implement public key cryptography in ways that are much more efficient than the traditional public key algorithms we have seen. It has been so successful that ECC implementations are often the default choice in modern cryptographic systems.

A major development in computing is the advent of quantum computers, machines that operate using the principles of quantum mechanics. Quantum computing could open new avenues in many different fields, including cryptography. For instance, quantum computers offer new ways to exchange keys securely, with security guaranteed by quantum mechanics. Quantum computers can use entirely new algorithms to solve mathematical problems, and it turns out that they can attack problems that are intractable with traditional computers. As modern cryptography rests on the difficulty of solving particular problems, we are heading for trouble if these problems can be solved effectively with quantum algorithms on quantum computers. In fact, we already know that this is exactly the case; some of our contemporary cryptographic methods, impregnable to today's machines, would be pregnable to quantum machines. Such machines do not yet exist; there are formidable engineering challenges to be solved before we can build quantum computers that can mount successful attacks. In the meantime, though, cryptographers have been developing post-quantum cryptography methods—that is, methods that will be invulnerable even when attacked by quantum computers.

This is a book on cryptography, and at its end it is appropriate to broach a wider subject: computer security. Cryptography allows us to secure our data and communication, but it is not enough. Secure computer systems use cryptography, but in order for a system to be truly secure a lot more must be taken into account. Implementations of algorithms must be correct, and that includes both software and hardware considerations. Perhaps most important, systems are designed, implemented, and used by people. Good cryptography is the first step in good security engineering, which is what can truly deliver what cryptography promises.

ECC

Our playthings have been numbers. In public key cryptography in particular, we saw how to encrypt, decrypt, and sign, with a series of arithmetic operations that work like everyday operations, yet with a twist: we take the remainder, that is the modulo, of the operation as the result.

If we take a step back, we can realize that even our familiar arithmetic operations are more multifaceted than we may think. We learn how to add natural numbers in primary school; once we master that, we learn how to add fractions. We call both operations "addition," but under the surface we apply different steps when adding two fractions than when adding two whole numbers. Some time later we may learn how to add yet other things, such as vectors in geometry or matrices in algebra.

What justifies using an umbrella term for the different kinds of addition is that for all of them, we use a more or less similar interpretation: combining, merging, or extending something with another. But not only that. To call something addition, it must satisfy a number of properties. Addition is *commutative*: for two elements a and b, $a + b = b + a$. It is *associative*: for three elements a, b, and c, $a + (b + c) = (a + b) + c$. It has an *identity element*, zero, such that the sum of the identity element with any element a is the same element: $a + 0 = a$. For each element a, there exists an element b, which we call its *inverse*, such that when we add it to a, we get the identity element: $a + b = 0$; we usually use $-a = b$ to denote the inverse of a.

We can therefore define an addition operation for entities other than numbers as long as the addition properties continue to hold. We would also require that the interpretation of the operation satisfy our notion of combining, merging, or extending, but mathematicians are happy to work with abstract entities where such everyday notions may apply at a stretch.

Let's see then how we can define addition for something quite different from numbers: points on specially selected curves. You can see two such curves in figures 51 and 52. The curve in figure 51 is the set of points with coordinates (x, y) that satisfy the equation $y^2 = x^3 - 2x + 2$. The curve in figure 52 is the set of points with coordinates (x, y) that satisfy the equation $y^2 = x^3 - 2x + 1$.

As you can see from figure 52, a curve need not be a single continuous line. In general, our curves will be of the form $y^2 = x^3 + ax + b$, where a and b are constants and the curve has no sharp corners, called cusps, or intersections, called nodes. In figures 53–54, you can see two curves that won't do; one with a cusp on the left, and one with a node on the right. A curve with cusps or nodes is called singular. We want nonsingular curves. Nonsingular curves meet the condition $4a^3 + 27b^2 \neq 0$, which you can check fails in figures 53–54.

The curves that meet our criteria are called *elliptic curves* even though, as you can see, they do not look like ellipses and should not be confused with them. The name comes from such equations being found in the study of the length of arcs of ellipses. Elliptic curves are a vibrant field of the theory of numbers. They are an important part of

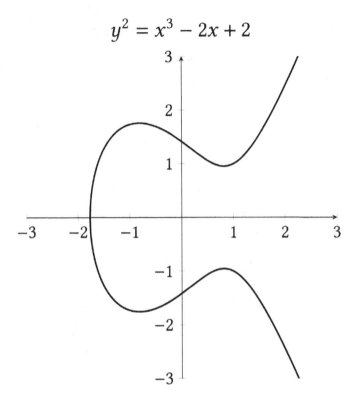

$$y^2 = x^3 - 2x + 2$$

Figure 51

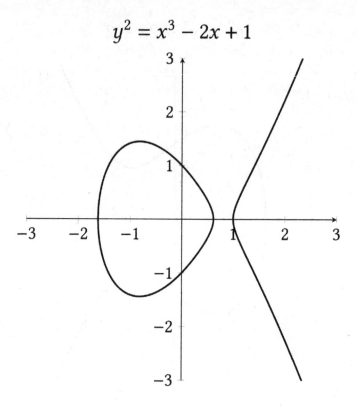

$$y^2 = x^3 - 2x + 1$$

Figure 52

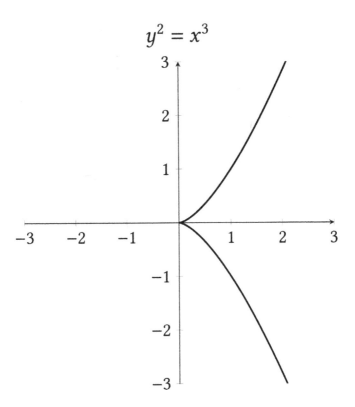

$$y^2 = x^3$$

Figure 53

$$y^2 = x^3 - 3x + 2$$

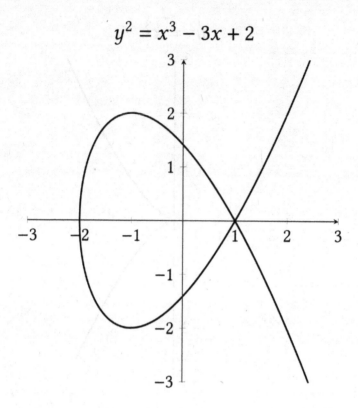

Figure 54

Andrew Wiles's proof of Fermat's last theorem, a proposition that Pierre de Fermat claimed to have proved around 1637. The proposition states that there are no distinct positive integers a, b, and c such that $a^n + b^n = c^n$ if $n > 2$. For $n = 2$ the equation holds, with an infinite number of possible solutions, per the Pythagorean theorem. Fermat's last theorem says that there is no generalization of the Pythagorean theorem for powers greater than 2 and positive integers a, b, c. Famously, Fermat commented that his proof was marvelous but could not fit on the margin of the page on which he was writing. That baffled mathematicians for centuries, until 1995 with Wiles's proof, which is more than a hundred pages long.

Having settled on the kind of curves that we will use, we need to define the addition of points on them. If we have two different points P and Q on a curve, we draw a line through P and Q. We find the intersection of the line with the curve. We then mirror the intersection along the x-axis. The mirrored point is the result of the addition $P + Q$. You can see the procedure, called the *chord rule*, in figure 55.

What if we want to add a point P to itself—that is, $P + P = 2P$? This is called point doubling. Since we do not have two distinct points to draw a line between them, we draw the tangent line on the curve through the point. We then find the intersection of the tangent line with the curve and take the mirror of the intersection along the x-axis as the point $2P$. This is called the *tangent rule*; see figure 56.

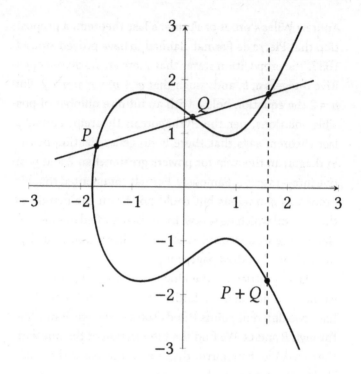

Figure 55

The operation that we have defined is both commutative and associative. We also need an identity element to meet all the properties required to function as addition. To find the identity element, we can observe that, in addition, it is equal to an element plus its inverse: $a + (-a) = 0$. If we take as the inverse of a point on the curve its mirror

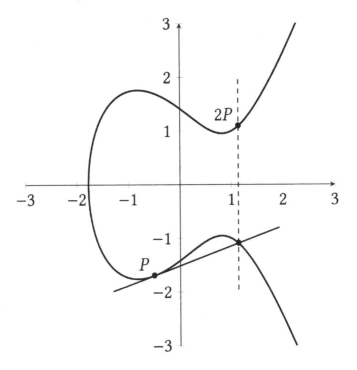

Figure 56

on the x-axis, then at first sight adding a point P and its inverse −P does not seem to work because the chord passing through them does not intersect the curve anywhere. You can see that for two points, P and Q, and their respective inverses, −P and −Q, in figure 57.

Well, in usual two-dimensional geometry, this is indeed so. We need to make a conceptual leap. See the railroad

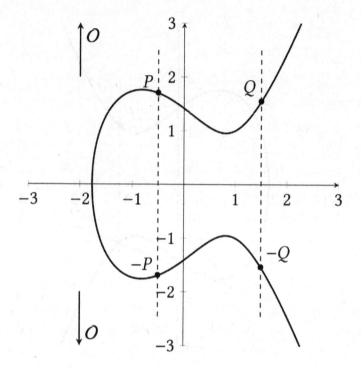

Figure 57

tracks in figure 58. The tracks are two parallel lines, yet, thanks to perspective, they seem to meet somewhere—to be more accurate, they meet at infinity. In a similar vein, we can imagine that all the parallel lines through points and their inverses, such as the line passing through P and $-P$ as well as the line passing through Q and $-Q$, meet at

Figure 58

infinity, both positive and negative, along the vertical y-axis. This *point at infinity* is our identity element; we denote it with $\mathcal{O}$ and have $P + (-P) = \mathcal{O}$, which entails $P + \mathcal{O} = P$. It is as if instead of a plane, we are working on a sphere. Think of the meridians on the globe, which meet at the north and south pole.

In reality, we do not need to work on a plot drawing curves, lines, and tangents. All the geometric operations we have described have their arithmetic equivalents, where we work with the coordinates of the points on the curves. We can add points easily, numerically. But there is a final turn we need to take. Working with curves in the way we have described gives results that are too predictable. Exactly because the curves are well behaved, we cannot hide our tracks on them: the result of adding two points has a straightforward geometric interpretation. We have already found the remedy. Rather than working with any point (x, y) on a curve, we take the points (x, y) that lie on the curve after applying a modulo operation. The result shows a chaos that should be familiar by now; in figure 59, you can see the curve $y^2 = x^3 - 2x + 2 \bmod 997$. Apart from the horizontal symmetry across the middle, which arises because the elliptic curve is symmetric along the horizontal axis, the points are no longer predictable.

We are now able to see how all of this fits together into ECC, which is public key cryptography based on elliptic curves. First we choose a curve—that is, the values a, b, and p for $y^2 = x^3 + ax + b \bmod p$. Then we can take a point P on the curve and add it to itself n number of times, arriving at a new point T:

$$\overbrace{P + P + \cdots + P}^{n} = nP = T$$

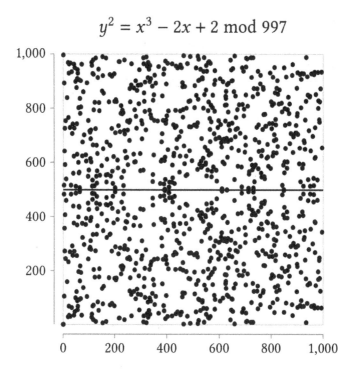

$$y^2 = x^3 - 2x + 2 \bmod 997$$

Figure 59

The *elliptic curve discrete logarithm problem* is to find the number n given the points P and T. As far as we know that is a difficult problem, as is the original discrete logarithm problem. We can try to find n by trying different values, but if n is large, this will not work in practice as it will take too long. "Elliptic curve discrete logarithm" is of course a misnomer because there is no logarithm involved. The name makes sense, though, if we realize that again it is difficult to reverse a repeated operation in modular arithmetic—only this time it is point addition instead of exponentiation.

If the elliptic curve discrete logarithm problem is hard, then we can use it for key exchange, in an analogy with the Diffie-Hellman key exchange that we have already encountered. Let's take Alice and Bob again, trying to agree on a secret value.

1. Alice and Bob agree on an elliptic curve they will use along with a starting point P.

2. Alice and Bob each pick up a number that they keep secret. Let's call Alice's secret a and Bob's secret b.

3. Alice computes the point $A = aP$, and Bob computes the point $B = bP$.

4. They send each other their results, not in secret.

5. Alice calculates the point $aB = a(bP)$, and Bob calculates the point $bA = b(aP)$. These two are the same point $T = a(bP) = b(aP)$. The coordinates of that point can be used as Alice's and Bob's secret.

The exchange is as in figure 60, which parallels figure 42 showing the Diffie-Hellman key exchange in chapter 3.

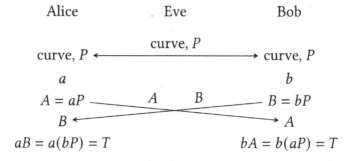

Figure 60

Apart from key exchange, other cryptographic protocols have been developed using elliptic curves so that we can use elliptic curves for generating signatures and hybrid encryption. The TLS protocol that we saw in the previous chapter can use ECC, and in fact current implementations do use elliptic curves.[1]

Here you may well ask, Why? It may be interesting that what we have been doing with plain numbers we can also do with more advanced mathematical techniques. But novelty is not a reason for rushing to adopt a new offering in cryptography. Quite the opposite, in fact: in matters of security and privacy, we are always better off adopting a conservative stance and sticking to what we know works and has withstood the test of time (and attacks). The fact that it *is* possible to use ECC does not automatically mean that we *ought* to use it.[2]

The answer to the question is that ECC, other things being equal, allows us to use shorter keys in our algorithms. Cryptographic operations can be executed faster with shorter keys, so our systems will require less time. Shorter keys also allow us to save space; a digital signature using elliptic curves will be smaller than an equivalent, in terms of security, that does not. And space may be of the essence in certain applications. For instance, if the digital signature is embedded in a QR code, which can be read and verified by a mobile device, the smaller it is, the easier it is to create an easy-to-read QR code.

We can get an idea of the savings we obtain by comparing RSA and elliptic curve cryptosystems. In all cryptographic systems, longer keys offer higher security, if only because trying to break them using a brute-force attack will take longer. An RSA key of length 2048 bits offers the security of an ECC key of 224–255 bits. If we want higher security and move to RSA keys of 3072 bits, the equivalent ECC keys in terms of security would have lengths of 256–383 bits. For even higher security, we can go to RSA keys of 7680 bits, with ECC going to 384–511 bits, or RSA with 15360 bits, equivalent to ECC with 512 bits.[3]

Such savings mean that often the default route to take is to go directly to an ECC implementation instead of using traditional arithmetic. That said, the route to the universal adoption of ECC has been bumpy. Cryptographers have worried that the NSA inserted a backdoor in the ECC standard for generating pseudorandom numbers; somebody with knowledge of the backdoor, which is a set of secret numbers, could predict the generated pseudorandom numbers and break protocols such as TLS. As with most things with three-letter agencies, we may never learn if the standard was intentionally weak or if the weakness was the result of unintentional oversight. Even without malicious intent, in order for ECC to be truly secure, it must work on carefully chosen elliptic curves. Just picking a curve satisfying the equation $y^2 = x^2 + ax + b$, as we have been blithely doing, may work for demonstration purposes but is a poor recipe for real-world security. Thankfully, cryptographers have risen to the task and have devoted time and effort to identifying elliptic curves that, to the best of our knowledge, we can have confidence are secure.[4]

Quantum Key Distribution

Richard P. Feynman, Nobel laureate in physics, remarked in a lecture at Cornell University in 1964, "I think I can safely say that nobody really understands quantum mechanics."[5] As he was awarded the Nobel prize for his work in quantum electrodynamics, a branch of quantum mechanics, we must take his observation seriously; he obviously knew what he was talking about. The problem with quantum theory is that it is strange and describes weird phenomena that conflict with our intuitions of how the physical world works (the problem of course lies with our intuitions, not with physics).

Feynman was also a pioneer in the early 1980s of the idea to harness quantum properties in order to build a more powerful kind of computer.[6] We will have more to say about that in the next section, but right now we will explore how exactly we can use the weirdness of quantum properties to perform a by-now-familiar task: exchanging cryptographic keys.

If you are familiar with sewing, you may have come across a needle compact. If you are not familiar, well, figure 61 offers a drawing of one.

A needle compact keeps the needles in place, as they can be inserted only in grooves on a disk. The disk's cover rotates and has a narrow slit through which we can put in or take out a needle. If the cover is rotated away from any of the needle positions, our needles are safe, as they cannot fall out. If we want to take out a particular needle (usually they come in different sizes), we can rotate the cover so that the slit is aligned with the needle we want to use. If we then tilt the needle compact with the slit facing downward, the needle will slip out.

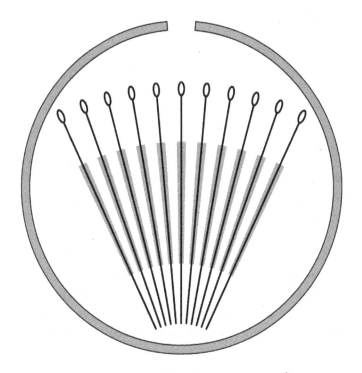

Figure 61

Let's take this idea a bit further and see how we can use an evolved needle compact to carry information in the form of binary digits. Our device will have four grooves. Two of them will be vertical and horizontal while the other two grooves will be orthogonal to each other but rotated by 45° with respect to the first pair. The device will have

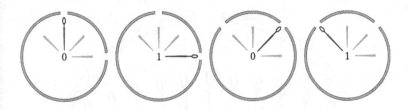

Figure 62

two slits instead of one, also orthogonal to each other. The slits can be aligned with any of the two pairs of orthogonal grooves.

We agree that if we slide a needle in the ↑ groove, our device carries the digit 0, while if we slide a needle in the → groove, our device carries the digit 1. Similarly, if we slide a needle along the ↗ groove, our device carries the digit 0, and if we slide a needle along the ↖ groove, our device carries the digit 1. For the possible configurations of our device, see figure 62.

Once the device is loaded with a needle, we turn the cover and cannot see from the outside which slit the needle has gone in. The only thing we can do with the device is rotate the slits and tilt it to see if a needle falls out. If the needle has been inserted in the ↑→ grooves and we align the slits along them, the needle will fall out from one of the two and we will know whether our device encodes a 0 or a 1. Similarly, if the needle has been inserted in the ↖↗ grooves and we align the slits along them, depending

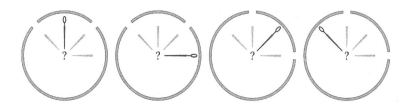

Figure 63

on the slit that the needle comes out, we will know if the device encodes a 0 or a 1.

But what if we don't align the slits along the right grooves, as in the situation in figure 63? Remember, once the device is loaded, we cannot see inside it. Well, if the slits are misaligned, then the needle can come out from either of them with equal chances. That means that we will get a 0 or a 1, but that will be correct only half of the time.

We can use such a device to exchange a key securely, as follows. We have our two characters, Alice and Bob. Alice decides on a random sequence of bits, 0s and 1s, that she wants to share with Bob. She puts each one of the bits in one of our devices and dispatches them to Bob. She keeps a record of the correct orientation of the slits in each device she dispatches. Bob does not know the correct orientation of the slits for each device he receives, so he picks one each time at random. He also records his choice.

As Bob does not know the correct orientation for decoding the contents of the devices he receives, his guess will be correct about half of the time, decoding half of the bits correctly—only he does not know which are the correctly decoded ones.

Once Bob has received all the devices from Alice, they send each other the orientations they have used. For Alice, that is the orientation of the slits that she used when encoding each bit in each device, and for Bob that is the orientation of the slits he used when decoding each bit in each device. Now Bob knows which of the bits he has decoded correctly, and he can simply keep them, as the secret key, and discard the others. Alice does the same: she knows which bits Bob decoded correctly, so she keeps them as the shared key and discards all the rest.

Let's see an example. In the first row of the following table, we have the random bits picked by Alice. The second row is Alice's slit orientations. The third row shows the needles inserted by Alice in the devices. Bob then receives the devices. Not knowing Alice's orientation choices, he makes up his own, shown in the fourth row, and therefore gets the needles as seen in the fifth row. These are decoded as bits, some of them correctly and some of them not, as in the sixth row. Alice and Bob then send to each other their respective orientations, rows two and four. Then they both know which bits were encoded and decoded correctly, and thus which ones to keep, shown in the last row. That is their shared secret key.

Alice's bits	1	0	1	0	0	1	1
Alice's orientation	↑→	↑→	↖↗	↖↗	↑→	↖↗	↑→
Alice's encoding	→	↑	↖	↗	↑	↖	→
Bob's orientation	↑→	↖↗	↖↗	↑→	↑→	↖↗	↖↗
Bob's decoding	→	↗	↖	→	↑	↖	↖
Bob's bits	1	0	1	1	0	1	1
Shared key	1		1		0	1	

This method for secret sharing is secure in the presence of Eve the eavesdropper. Eve may intercept the devices and open them; like Bob, she will have no idea of the correct orientations and whether her decoding is in fact correct. But she will have to reinsert the needle in each device and send it on its way to Bob. As she does not know the correct orientation of the slits for each device, however, she will have to use her own choice, which will be correct about half of the time. That means that the devices she forwards to Bob will have the same slit orientation as the ones she received from Alice only half of the time. This in turn means that when Alice and Bob compare notes, if Eve has indeed intercepted their devices, Alice and Bob will discover that, half of the time, the slit orientations picked by Alice are not the ones received by Bob. This indicates that interception has taken place, and Alice and Bob know that the key is compromised. Secret sharing using our devices is secure because it is impossible to intercept the secrets in a way that the interception will not be detected.

We have been talking about needles and grooves, but the procedure for creating a key exchange mechanism like the one we have described relies on quantum physics. Instead of needles, we use photons to encode our bits. The photons can be encoded in two different ways, called *bases*, orthogonal to each other. Like our needles, if we use the correct base, we get the correct encoding of the bit. If we use the other base, we will get the correct encoding only half of the time. And once a photon is decoded, it is spent. Eve, if she intercepts the photon, will have to send Bob a new set of encoded photons—but she does not know the correct base to encode each one of them.

This *quantum key distribution* (QKD) is an example of *quantum cryptography*, the application of quantum properties for cryptographic purposes. Quantum properties are widely held to be bizarre because at the quantum level, the world behaves differently from our everyday experience. For instance, we cannot always be sure of the outcome of a measurement, as the result will be probabilistic. We see that in the quantum key exchange: if we do not pick the correct base, we will decode a binary value from each encoded photon but the value will be arbitrary. Only if we pick the right base will the decoding be equal to the encoding, and we have no indication of what the correct base is.

Working with quantum properties, though, is not straightforward. Quantum cryptography works on a different set of assumptions than cryptography as we have seen it to this point. Instead of security being provided through mathematics, in quantum cryptography security is provided through physics. That brings new kinds of limitations; for example, while key exchange mechanisms like Diffie-Hellman can work on any network, over any distance, QKD can work only on special communication links and special-purpose equipment. Also, QKD can solve a particular problem, that of exchanging keys, but that is only part of the whole problem that needs to be solved for secure communications. We have seen that you must be able to authenticate the party with whom you are communicating too. It makes little sense to exchange a key securely with an impostor, and QKD does not authenticate the communicating partners. QKD by itself does not guarantee security.[7]

That points to a wider issue. People often conflate cryptography with security. That is simply wrong. Cryptography can give us the theoretical means with which to achieve security. But security requires constructing systems that work in the real world, not in the ideal one of mathematics and physics. Real-world systems require substantial engineering effort and encompass not just technology but people as well. We will return to the relationship between security and cryptography in a little bit, but first let's explore another angle of quantum physics and cryptography.

Post-Quantum Cryptography

We have seen, time and again, that modern cryptography rests on mathematics. The algorithms are secure because to break them we need to solve mathematical problems that, as things currently stand, we do not know how to solve efficiently. The security of the Diffie-Hellman key exchange depends on the difficulty of solving the discrete logarithm problem. The security of RSA relies on the difficulty of factoring large prime numbers.

If these problems were solved by some stroke of genius, cryptographic methods that are based on them would no longer be secure. Up to this point, such a stroke of genius has not occurred. A different threat, however, has appeared with the advent of quantum computing.

Quantum computing is a big subject on its own. Broadly speaking, it is the application of quantum physics for performing computations. A basic feature of quantum computing is that we no longer work on binary digits or bits, but rather on quantum bits called *qubits*. While a bit can exist in two states, 0 or 1, a qubit can exist in what is called a *superposition* of the two states. Far be it from us to delve into the wonders of quantum physics; suffice it to say that, in a way, a qubit can represent both 0 and 1 simultaneously. Only when we measure it will its state collapse to a single 0 or 1. But until we do measure it, we can manipulate it as if we were manipulating both possible outcomes at the same time.

This results, in theory at least, in computers that can solve computational problems much faster than classical (meaning non-quantum) computers. Note the "in theory" weasel words. Building quantum computers is not easy; there are still formidable technological challenges that prevent us from constructing quantum computers with enormous computational power. A major challenge to harnessing the potential of quantum computing is inventing *quantum algorithms* that leverage the properties of qubits to perform calculations faster than classical (meaning non-quantum) computers. Quantum algorithms offer the tantalizing prospect of undercutting the theoretical time limitations of classical algorithms. Such algorithms do exist.

One such algorithm was published in 1994 by US mathematician Peter Shor. The algorithm can be used to factor primes and find discrete logarithms on quantum computers much more efficiently than on classical computers. Shor's algorithm is a cornerstone of quantum computation. If sufficiently powerful quantum computers are built, cryptographic systems like Diffie-Hellman and RSA will be powerless against attacks, as it will be possible to derive their secret keys.

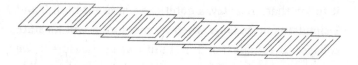

Figure 64

It is not just public key encryption that is vulnerable to quantum computers. Asymmetric algorithms, like AES, can be attacked, although not as severely, by quantum computers. That's because searching for a key with a brute-force method is less prohibitive when we move over to quantum algorithms.

If you want to search for an item among n items, which are not in any particular order, in the worst case you have to examine each one of them. Suppose you have a deck of index cards and are trying to find a particular card among them. If the pack is not sorted in any way, you can start examining each card one by one, in any order you choose, until you come on the one you seek, as in figure 64. If you are unlucky, this may be the last card in the pack, so in the worst case, for n cards, you need n operations—that is, checks. This *sequential search* algorithm is the best we can do with classical means.

Now imagine that we have a magic wand we can pass over our deck of n cards. When the wand passes over the deck, the card that we are looking for moves outward a bit. If we move our wand over the deck $\sqrt{n}$ times, then the

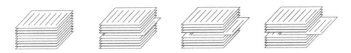

Figure 65

card will stand out far enough that it is easy for us to pick it up, as seen in figure 65.

In real life, magic wands that perform such feats do not exist. But an algorithm developed by Indian American computer scientist Lov Grover in 1996 uses quantum properties to identify one out of n items in no more than $\sqrt{n}$ steps. Grover's algorithm, the second major quantum computing algorithm after Shor's, works iteratively. In each iteration, the quantum state of the qubits is changed so that when we measure the outcome after $\sqrt{n}$ iterations, we will get the value that corresponds to the item we are looking for.[8]

In AES, if we use a key of 128 bits, an attacker would need up to 2^{128} efforts to break it by brute force—that is, by trying to guess it. Grover's algorithm can be used to find the correct key among all the possible keys, as this is akin to searching for one item among a pile of other items. AES is secure because by brute force, it is infeasible to find the needle in the proverbial haystack. Using Grover's algorithm, however, the haystack can be winnowed down considerably. The number of steps to guess an AES key of 128 bits would go down to 2^{64}. That is not as severe as Shor's effect on RSA and Diffie-Hellman, but it does bring our security guarantees down a peg (or, rather, $\sqrt{n}$ pegs down).

Thanks to our current technological limitations, we are safe for now, but that is a rather disquieting state of affairs. Engineers work hard on the hardware problems surrounding quantum computers. After some time we may have quantum computers powerful enough to use Shor's algorithm, Grover's algorithm, or some other quantum algorithm and break the actual cryptographic systems that we use today. And that is not a problem only for future generations—to whom humans are particularly adept at kicking the can down the road. In the future, quantum computers may break today's secrets, not just those of the future. Any communications, messages, files, and documents that we have encrypted with a method we deem safe today, yet will not be safe against quantum computers, will become vulnerable. This threat is called *store-now-decrypt-later*. An adversary may simply hoard state secrets, confidential trade documents, medical records, or any other sensitive and at present safely encrypted information. True, even state secrets are declassified and released from the archives to become part of history after sufficient time has passed. Here, though, we are not faced with any choice: encrypted secrets will no longer be safe because the mechanisms we have been using to lock them have come unlocked.

Enter *post-quantum cryptography* (PQC): cryptography that works even under the assumption that powerful quantum computers are available. Faced with the specter of quantum computing, cryptographers have been busy: first, studying which of our cryptographic methods will be at risk; and second, developing other cryptographic solutions that, as far as we know, are immune to attacks by quantum computers.[9]

Regarding symmetric cryptography, the solution is pretty straightforward: use longer keys, like 256 bit keys in AES. For asymmetric cryptography, where Shor's algorithm can be devastating when run on a capable quantum computer, salvation comes through the use of other algorithms that are quantum resistant. *Code-based encryption*, *lattice-based encryption*, *hash-based cryptography*, and *supersingular elliptic curve isogeny* (the underlying mathematics may be gnarled, but the names are poetic) are approaches that are immune to known quantum computing algorithms.

From these approaches, lattice-based encryption has an appealing and straightforward geometric interpretation. Let's start with the name itself. A *lattice* is a mathematical construct, which can be interpreted as a set of points that has a crystalline structure, like in the left side of figure 66.[10]

Two lattice points cannot be closer than some minimum distance, and every point is no further away than

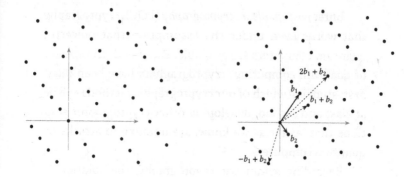

Figure 66

some maximum distance from a lattice point. If we add or subtract the coordinates of two points, we'll get to another point in the lattice. In algebra, a point is equivalent to a directed segment—that is, a *vector*—from the point of origin. A lattice is then the set of points that is produced by adding and subtracting multiples of a set of chosen vectors, called *basis vectors*. On the right side of the figure, you can see that the lattice is produced by these operations on the basis vectors b_1 and b_2.

Even though the image shows a two-dimensional lattice in a plane, lattices can exist in any number of dimensions; however, it is difficult to visualize a three-dimensional lattice, let alone going up to higher dimensions. A lattice in n dimensions is produced by n vectors.

Given a lattice, the *closest vector problem* (CVP) is to find the point in the lattice that is closest to another point

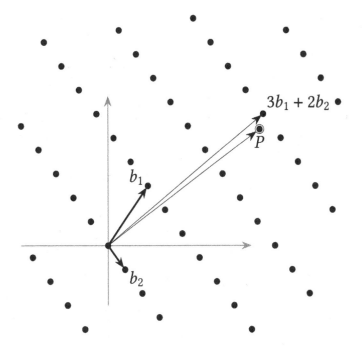

Figure 67

that is not necessarily on the lattice. In other words, to find a vector in the lattice that is closest to another vector, which may not be in the lattice. In the following image, given the point or vector P, we have to find the closest lattice point to it, which is $3b_1 + 2b_2$, as seen in figure 67.

In two dimensions, the problem may appear simple, but appearances are deceptive when we move to more dimensions. In practice, we work with hundreds of dimensions. The difficulty of solving the CVP underpins lattice-based PQC. In contrast to factoring large prime numbers, however, we know of no quantum algorithm that could solve the CVP problem effectively.

To promote the development of post-quantum approaches, NIST announced in 2016 the Post-Quantum Cryptography Standardization, a competition to identify and propose standards for PQC. The competition runs in rounds. In the first round, eighty-two submissions from twenty-five countries were received. On January 30, 2019, twenty-six candidates made it to the second round. On July 22, 2020, seven finalists and eight alternate candidates were selected to move to the third round. Just shy of two years later, on July 5, 2022, NIST announced the first group of four winners of the competition and four candidates to be evaluated in round four.

Shortly after the announcement of the round four candidates, two researchers, Wouter Castryck and Thomas Decru from Katholieke Universiteit Leuven in Belgium, published an efficient attack on the scheme underlying one of them, called SIKE. Breaking the system took anywhere from sixty-two minutes to twenty hours and thirty-seven minutes, depending on the hardness of the setup. No fancy hardware was needed; these times were on a traditional computer, not a quantum one, with a single core. The attack was practical and relied on using advanced mathematics.[11]

In a certain way, we come back to the lock competitions we saw in the chapter 2. Recall that NIST spearheaded the development of a modern secure symmetric encryption algorithm by running an open competition that gave us AES. PQC evolves in a similar vein. Once more, the best way to security is not through obscurity; in cryptography, we place our confidence in those solutions that have passed muster with the cryptographic community. By putting their cards on the table, cryptographers assure us that their locks are as secure as we can know them to be.

Threat Models and Provable Security

Cryptography can appear like a cat-and-mouse game. A cipher is proposed, and attacks are sought; if it's found to be vulnerable without remedy, it will be abandoned and a new, hopefully better cipher will be developed, and so on and so forth. The value of a cryptographic method accumulates with the number of unsuccessful efforts that have been made to break it.

That is true, but it does not mean that cryptographers do not aim for additional ways to ensure their inventions are secure. These are based on more precise, and even formal, definitions of attacks and security.

Instead of talking about attacks in general, we can recognize particular kinds of attacks, or *threat models*, and examine how an encryption scheme behaves against them. These threat models assume that the attacker has some particular capabilities. We have already seen a couple of these models previously, which we'll now include in a scale of threat models, corresponding to increasing power on the part of the attacker.

The least powerful form of attack is the *ciphertext-only attack*, where we assume that the attacker only has access to a set of one or more ciphertexts. From this set, the attacker tries to glean information on the underlying plaintext or plaintexts. We saw this kind of attack in practice in classical cryptography. Old ciphers could be broken with frequency analysis using only ciphertexts to find the encryption key.

If the attacker has access not only to a set of one or more ciphertexts but to a set of known plaintext and ciphertext pairs as well, then we move on to the known-plaintext attack, which we saw was used to break the Enigma at Bletchley Park.

The attacker is more powerful when able to use plaintext and ciphertexts pairs for *plaintexts of their choice*, which leads us to the *chosen plaintext attack*. An example of this comes, again, from World War II. During the war in the Pacific, the US Navy cryptanalysts partially decrypted a message indicating that the Japanese were planning an attack at "AF." Even though it was suspected that "AF" referred to the Midway atoll, military planners in Washington were not convinced. Some confirmation was needed. To obtain it, the navy cryptanalysts drafted a message in which Midway reported that its fresh-water distillation plant had broken down. They cabled the message to Midway, with instructions to report it back over radio in clear (not in code), so that it could be intercepted by the Japanese. Then they waited. Two days later, among the Japanese messages that were intercepted, one stated that "AF" was short of water. The location of the oncoming attack was revealed. The Battle of Midway, won by the Americans, was a turning point in the war.[12]

Finally, if the attacker is able to use plaintext and ciphertext pairs for *ciphertexts of their choice* we arrive at the chosen ciphertext attack, which we saw can be mounted against the CTR mode in symmetric encryption.

Although each one of these attacks is more powerful than the others, it does not mean that it is better than the others. It depends on what we want to achieve; we choose the attack model that suits the environment of the encryption scheme. A more powerful attack, like chosen ciphertext attack, may simply not be applicable if we cannot get plaintext and ciphertext pairs for chosen ciphertexts. Having defined these models, instead of talking abstractly about possible attacks, we can evaluate the encryption scheme against possible attacks launched by an attacker with the capabilities afforded by the specific threat model.

Assessing the security of a cipher by trying to break it in different ways is called *heuristic security*. In computer science, heuristic approaches (from the Greek εὑρίσκω, *heurískō*, which means "to find") are practical methods that rely on informal strategies, like trial and error and rules learned from experience. Heuristic methods are neither based on rigorous proofs nor guaranteed to produce the optimal outcome, but often they are the best we can do to tackle a problem.

That does not mean that we don't aim at the optimal outcome and at having methods that are based on rigorous mathematical proofs. In cryptography, that is the aim of *provable security*. Our goal in provable security is to produce a proof that a cryptographic construction satisfies certain guarantees, based on particular assumptions.

We have treated provable security without calling it by name. Provable security proofs can be of the form "this cryptographic construction is at least as difficult to break as it is to solve this hard mathematical problem." Or to be more precise, "this cryptographic construction is immune from an attack of type X provided that the mathematical problem Y is computationally hard." We saw that Diffie-Hellman rests on the difficulty of finding discrete logarithms, and that RSA relies on the difficulty of factoring large numbers.

The mathematical technique used in such proofs is called *reduction* because it entails reducing one problem to another. Reduction is an important tool in theoretical computer science, where we try to compare and classify problems according to their computational difficulty. In provable security, reduction means that if an adversary found a method to mount a successful attack against a cryptographic system, we could transform this method into an efficient algorithm that would solve a computationally hard problem. For example, if an attacker finds a method to break RSA, then we would be able to factor large integers efficiently with little extra effort. Since we do not believe that to be feasible, we also believe that we will not be able to break RSA.

Provable security is an essential part of modern cryptography. It is definitely commendable to propose cryptographic systems with a rigorous security proof instead of relying on intuition. That said, it is important to keep in mind that provable security is not the same as *real-world security*. A system can be provably secure yet broken in a different way; for instance, the implementation may be sloppy or the attacker may find a whole different line of attack that circumvents the hard computational problem. Moreover, from a mathematical point of view, a particular hard computational problem may not remain hard forever. Unless there is proof that the problem cannot be solved efficiently, we may be able to solve it efficiently in the future. There is no proof that the discrete logarithm problem cannot be solved by an efficient algorithm, and the same goes for factoring. We believe that it's unlikely, but we cannot be certain. And we saw that other developments, like quantum computing, may soften the hardness of problems.

A related problem is that cryptographic proofs can just be wrong. They can be long and complicated. Usually they are peer reviewed, so we trust that any flaws will be revealed in the review process. But that may not always happen, and errors in cryptographic constructions have been discovered following their publication. Cryptographic systems whose descriptions run tens of pages, impenetrable to the uninitiated, may also be difficult to implement for real-world production use (as opposed to a simple proof of concept). When the author, a computer scientist by training, had to implement such systems, the only way to do that (no doubt because he is not clever enough) was to sit down with the cryptographers who had invented the systems and written their proofs, and go step-by-step to figure out how to implement the algorithms in working code.

Neal Koblitz, one of the creators of ECC, threw this into sharp relief when he published a scathing critique of provable security in the September 2007 issue of the respected *Notices of the American Mathematical Society*. Researchers responded by writing letters to the journal, calling the article "snobbery at its purest," and urging that "one should continue research, implementation and interaction, instead of slander."[13] Despite the bitterness, such altercations may help to promote progress by highlighting the need for a middle ground. Theoreticians and practitioners must work together to strengthen the security guarantees of a system, and each should be modest about their role and the assurances they can provide.[14]

All of this does not mean that we should disparage provable security, but it does mean that we have to widen our scope when talking about the real security afforded by a system.

Computer Security

We have touched on security several times in this book; we want our cryptographic systems to be secure so that they keep our secrets. But cryptography is only a part of the wider picture of computer security.

Cryptography gives us blueprints in the form of algorithms based on mathematics. These blueprints can help us protect our data, keep our communications confidential, and safeguard our privacy. But the blueprints by themselves do not achieve any of these things. They must be implemented in actual working tools embedded in systems that we can use.

A system encompasses much more than cryptographic methods. Cryptography must run on some hardware. The hardware can include embedded sensors, cell phones, laptops and personal computers, network equipment, communications infrastructure, computers running on data centers, computational and storage resources on the cloud, and high-performance computers. In order to operate, all hardware needs an operating system, and then on top of the operating system, we have the actual applications that we are using, be they for banking, health, chat, video calls, and so on.

A system goes beyond software and hardware, comprising human beings as well. These may be technical staff, such as system administrators, technicians, and various other technology professionals who are essential for the system to operate. These people rarely operate in a vacuum. They work in enterprises and organizations, so the system encompasses other employees and collaborators too. Finally we reach the outer perimeter of the system where it touches the external users of the systems—for instance, Alice and Bob when they want to chat privately.

The whole system is as secure as its weakest link, and any of the above can be, and are, targets of attack. Cryptography itself is rarely the weakest link. In terms of vulnerability, mathematics is nearly invincible. Once something has been proven correct, it is correct, unless some flaw is discovered in the proof (extremely unlikely) or an attack using some other mathematical technique is found—which takes a lot of ingenuity and effort. Algorithms also come with proofs of correctness. Mathematical and algorithmic proofs are like Platonic ideals: they are in a way perfect, existing in a higher form of reality.

Problems start when we move from an abstract world of ideas to our base, everyday existence. To use a modern cryptographic method, we have to write a computer program implementing the algorithms of the method. In contrast to an algorithm, we cannot be sure that a program is correct. Quite the contrary, programs start their lives full of errors, bugs, that programmers fix as they are found. Testing programs to locate bugs is a fundamental part of software development, and yet there is always the chance that a bug will escape and find its way out in a working system. Sometimes big media outlets report on important security incidents that arise from the discovery of bugs in widely used systems. In technical parlance, a bug—or in more general terms, a weakness—is a *vulnerability*; once this results in an actual breach of security, we have an *incident*. There are international processes and guidelines for reporting incidents and vulnerabilities so that users are warned and fixes are rolled out as quickly as possible. Particularly pernicious are *zero-day* vulnerabilities—that is, vulnerabilities that are unknown to those who would like to fix them, like the makers of a software application. When a zero-day vulnerability is found, there is by definition no known fix for it, so the targeted system is vulnerable for the time it will take to be fixed, called the *window of vulnerability*.

Zero-day vulnerabilities have an ethical dimension. If they are discovered by a benevolent actor, should they inform the makers of the vulnerable system or should they warn everybody? If it is likely that nobody else knows about the vulnerability, it makes sense to inform those who can fix it and give them adequate time to respond before announcing the vulnerability publicly. If it is made public after a fix has been found, then by that time it will have been neutralized. Unfortunately, the vulnerability may already be known to malevolent actors and postponing public disclosure may afford them more time to take advantage of it—better then to warn users immediately. Warning those who can fix the bug and giving them sufficient time to fix it before announcing the vulnerability to the public is called *coordinated vulnerability disclosure* or *responsible disclosure*, and is often the most sensible way, but as you can imagine there are arguments for both options.

Even if a program implements a cryptographic method correctly and the cryptographic method is secure, attacks on the system can still be mounted using auxiliary sources of information via what is called a *side-channel attack*. It is possible to glean details of a cryptographic implementation using such sources as the power consumption of the system, leaked electromagnetic radiation, the time it takes to perform various operations, acoustic analysis of keyboard strokes, finger taps on a screen, or sound emanations from a computer.[15] If it seems that anything is up for grabs, that's because it really is. Any information that can be gathered from a system can be used against it, and researchers have shown a lot of creativity in finding such sources of information.

Computer security becomes more fraught once we take into account people: often, humans are the weakest link in the system. Instead of trying to break a password, it is much easier to try to guess it. We are regularly told to use strong passwords, whose strength is commensurate with how long and random they are. Unfortunately, strong passwords are generally difficult to remember. Worse, if we are asked to change our passwords every few months, then we are more and more tempted to just write them down somewhere (from where they can be stolen), or we end up using something easy to remember but also easy to guess by an attacker. Services may, instead of passwords, use some biometric data, like our face. Such technologies are not universally available or applicable, so they coexist with passwords rather than completely replacing them. Other authentication schemes rely on some special hardware, usually a cryptographic device that holds our key

Computer security becomes more fraught once we take into account people: often, humans are the weakest link in the system.

and with which we connect to a computer, but then some-body might steal that hardware.

Even if we do everything with our outmost diligence, "hell," as Jean-Paul Sartre wrote in his 1944 play *Huis clos* (*No Exit*), "is other people." Our confidential information may be stored securely by a company. Then the issue is who actually has access to that information apart from us. Companies must have security policies dictating exactly who has access to what and under which circumstances. Making sure that security policies are implemented cor-rectly is an organizational problem, not a technical one. If something goes wrong with the security policy, the wrong people may have access to our data.

Most of the time, though, our worst enemy is our-selves. We trust each other, and with good reason. Without trust, societies cannot function properly, and the vast ma-jority of the people we encounter are not out there to get us. Which means that the easiest way to break a system is simply to dupe people. This is called *social engineering* and can be wildly successful. We receive emails and messages with news that is too good to be true, like an inheritance that waits for us from some unknown relative, if only we part with some money or our credit card details. We get messages with alluring links, but woe betide anybody who actually follows such links. And these are the obvious at-tacks. What if we get an actual phone call from our bank asking us to verify some of our information? What if, as the call goes on, the information it needs to check includes our password?

Sometimes no attack is necessary. People themselves are willing to give their own personal information, just to get their job done. As a personal note in this book, over the years the author has been responsible for several sensitive services. It has never ceased to amaze him how eager users are to offer their private data, unasked, when they have trouble using the system and believe that this will help crack the problem and make the system behave as they believe it should.[16]

Computer security is hard—much harder than cryptography. True, you cannot have security without cryptography. Good cryptography is a necessary condition, but not a sufficient one. Computer security is about securing systems and *security engineering* is a whole fascinating subject on its own.[17]

EPILOGUE

In November 2022, a friend of mine, a journalist, called me about a sensitive matter. My home country, Greece, was reeling under the revelations that its National Intelligence Service had been running a wiretapping operation, installing spyware in the cell phones of individuals. She had suspicions that her phone had been hacked. We arranged for her to come over to my office and try to find out what we could.[1]

The spyware under question was called Predator. An open-source package, the Mobile Verification Toolkit (MVT), can scan the contents of a cell phone for traces of Predator hacking. I thought it would be a good idea to learn how to use MVT by checking my own phone before my friend's, which I did, and it came out clean.

She came as planned, and we started the scanning process. That takes some time, and you monitor the progress on your computer's screen. We took the opportunity to catch up. While we were waiting for the scan to end, exchanging chitchat, I was keeping an eye on the screen. Then something happened. The continuous scroll of lines showing the progress of the scanning changed; instead of a hypnotic roll of uneventful messages, warnings began to appear.

I froze and let out an expletive, at which point my friend also stopped talking and asked what was going on. I uttered, staccato style, something like, "Yes, it is. Hacked. Your phone." I do not recall my words exactly. But what I do remember is the acutely awkward feeling between my realization of what had happened and my turning to answer her. I am not a medical doctor, but perhaps that was what doctors feel like when they are about to tell a patient that they are terminally ill. And the realization dawned on me that security and privacy is not just an abstract notion, nor an academic field or line of work, but rather something deeply personal. We may know something well, but only when we experience it in our guts do we truly understand it.

My discomfort of course paled in comparison to what she felt: hurt, dismayed, and aghast, as she had every reason to be. Burglary leaves a trauma because we cannot accept that somebody has invaded our personal space and rummaged through our things. Today, most of our personal experiences are recorded on our cell phones. Breaking into them means somebody has gotten access to just about everything we do—trivial or significant, professional or personal. And it's actually worse than a break-in because it's difficult or even impossible to know what the intruder did once inside. We also don't know where this stops. A burglar will pass on stolen goods to a fence. An intruder can copy whatever they find and pass it on to who knows, who can again copy and pass it on, and so on. We bristle at the knave who has violated our personal space. How much worse when all of our lives, not just our physical surroundings, have been defiled and could turn up anywhere.

I hope the reader will forgive the author for this stab at a memoir, but we should not lose sight of the fact that cryptography is not about technology, nor is it about mathematics; it is about real people and actual lives. We have not had the opportunity to explore such themes in this book so far, but we should not reach the end before we do.

At the heart of the matter is a question of power. Cryptography provides security, and the provision of security is among the justifications for authority.[2] Governments are expected to keep their subjects safe. Even the war machine is always about defense; the author knows of no Ministry of Attack, but plenty of Ministries of Defense around the world (but plainly, in any conflict somebody has to attack, so something is fishy here).

Cryptography has over time been treated as an important factor in national security. Governments have tried to control the use and spread of cryptographic tools. For

At the heart of the matter is a question of power. Cryptography provides security, and the provision of security is among the justifications for authority.

instance, until the 1990s, cryptography in the United States was subject to strict export controls. This led to some bizarre situations. A best-selling book on cryptography and the point of entry for many people in the field was Bruce Schneier's *Applied Cryptography*. In the second edition of the book (1996), part V, at the end, consists of pages and pages of source code in the C programming language implementing the material of the preceding chapters. Why go into the trouble of printing that amount of source code when it could be distributed in some digital format (like a disk, which was used to accompany books back then)? After all, having to type by hand source code read from a book is hardly practical. The answer is that the controls at the time would not allow the export of cryptographic material in digital format outside the United States, but printed matter was exempt.

An even more absurd situation concerned the distribution of the software package Pretty Good Privacy (PGP), one of the first cryptographic tools that was targeted at the wider computer-literate public. PGP could not be exported from the United States. To get around the problem, the whole source code of the software was printed out and sent to Europe, where it was scanned and used to reconstitute the working program.

Today most export restrictions have been dropped, but not all. Some still remain, dealing with exports to places that are categorized as rogue states and terrorist organizations. But if cryptographic tools are nowadays widely available, the question of control remains on a different, more technical aspect.

The issue is whether, under certain circumstances, authorities should be able to bypass the protections afforded by cryptography. This can mean that cryptographic tools should have backdoors so that when the need arises, some officials will be able to bypass their security and directly decrypt ciphertexts without having to break the system. Or it may require that some encryption tools also have some kind of master key that is known to authorities and can be used to open ciphertexts when required. The argument for such backdoors is, again, based on security and cannot be waved away. For example, having access to the communication between the members of a terrorist cell can be essential to preventing serious harm and loss of life.

There are, however, two problems with the contention. First, there may be other, more traditional ways to keep an eye on suspicious activity (secret agents are supposed to do that). Second, once a backdoor exists in a cryptographic product, it is difficult to ensure that it will only be used and not abused. When surveillance scandals erupt, we often learn that the surveillance net had been cast far wider than one would have thought. We are not really surprised that governments do surveil people; what usually surprises us is the particular people we learn are the targets of surveillance, when we feel that they shouldn't be.

This is summed up with the familiar phrase "Who watches the watchers?" or "Quis custodiet ipsos custodes?" in the original Latin. Even though the phrase seems to be pregnant with political overtones, it was written in a different context, in a satirical poem by Roman poet Juvenal (first–second century CE). While Roman men were busy running the empire, the womenfolk were mostly at home. There they would be guarded to avoid any marital infidelities, but Juvenal was worried: How could one be sure that no happy carouses broke out between the women and the guardians themselves?

More seriously, in the context of political power, the issue had been raised earlier in Plato's *Republic* (written about 375 BCE). The *Republic* is perhaps Plato's best-known work, and one of the most influential works of philosophy and political science of all time. Plato describes the ideal city, in which a special social class, called the guardians, would be responsible for ensuring that the rules and norms of the society were followed. Like the rest of Plato's books, the *Republic* is written as a dialogue with Socrates. As the dialogue progresses, the question is posed, How could we ensure that the guardians are acting rightly? The answer, given by Glaucon, one of Socrates's interlocutors, is that "it would be absurd that a guardian should need a guard."[3]

That is not entirely satisfying, as it really entails accepting that we somehow have guardians who are immaculate.

But humans are never perfect. It is not just that we should be worried an authoritarian government will abuse its power to monitor its citizens. A more prosaic risk is that, unfortunately, humans can be venal. If backdoors to a system exist, it is not necessary that we fall prey to state actors. We may simply fall victim to racketeering and extortion by corrupt officials, government employees, and contractors that have access to the backdoors.

This indicates that if backdoors exist, there must be appropriate systems and processes that govern their use. We should not rely on the integrity of powerful individuals but instead have checks and balances in place. Even though it is a technical matter, that is not a reason why informed citizens should not have an opinion, particularly as the issue will be raised again and again as technology evolves. It is unfortunate that such discussions can become heated. Fear is a primal emotion, necessary for our survival, but subject to manipulation, and the powers that be know that fear is a time-tested method to keep the rabble in line.[4]

That is not to disparage experts, without which the discipline would not exist. Arguments to dispense with experts usually smack of populism. Computer scientists, security researchers, and cryptographers do have a special role in the discussion as they provide the material and set the scene. But technical expertise does not translate to any special prerogative in the social and political realms. Nowadays, there is anticipation and trepidation about the possible emergence of artificial general intelligence (AGI) that will surpass human intelligence. Until that happens (if ever), we can joke and recognize that there is no all-around genius individual (again AGI) who is wise in every human endeavor. A brilliant scientist may be a complete ignoramus in social matters, and the problems in which scientists engage are very much the products of their time. Isaac Newton is surely one of the greatest scientists who has ever lived. Apart from ushering in modern physics, he spent a considerable amount of time researching alchemy, looking for the sacred geometry of the Temple of Solomon, exploring biblical chronology, investigating the potential for the philosopher's stone, and other kinds of occult studies. Perhaps if he had stuck to physics, we would be a couple centuries more advanced in our scientific knowledge now, but Newton believed that this alternative line of research was his most important work.[5] Everybody is fallible, but hopefully not at the same time—that being a reason for holding wide consultations.

Controlling cryptography is not only about political power and national security. Cryptographic tools can be and are wielded by criminals. *Malware* is software that is intentionally designed to cause harm. A special kind of malware, *ransomware*, uses cryptography to block access to data until a ransom is paid. It encrypts data and requires a ransom payment in order to decrypt information or release the key used for decryption. By using a

Controlling cryptography is not only about political power and national security. Cryptographic tools can be and are wielded by criminals.

strong cryptographic method, malware can lock users out of their own computers. The effects can be catastrophic. In one famous incident, on May 14, 2021, the Health Service Executive of Ireland suffered a major malware attack that caused all of its information systems nationwide to shut down. Hospital work was disrupted. The Irish state refused to pay the ransom, and it took weeks for the systems to be restored.[6]

That indicates that attitudes toward the control of cryptography may be nuanced. The same person who balks at governments being able to bypass cryptographic systems for surveillance purposes may welcome being able to overcome criminal attacks affecting thousands of innocent and sick people. At the same time, the very existence of malware brings in a host of questions on the moral dimension of cryptography.

The first ransomware was invented and presented in a scientific conference in 1996 by two cryptography researchers. In 2017, they remarked that it had taken more than twenty years for cryptography-based extortion to attract widespread attention, and that possible attacks, fully described in the scientific literature, were still being overlooked as a large-scale, real-world attack had not yet emerged.[7] Should the researchers have described the attack in the first place? Does it make sense to argue that cryptographers should not publish possible attacks in general? Isn't it better that we know about them, rather than finding out when an attack breaks out and we are caught completely unprepared?

It is naive to believe that cryptography is disengaged from political and social issues. We would then expect that cryptographers adopt an ethic of responsibility. On the one hand, they ought not to inflict evil or harm: scientists and engineers should refrain from work that damages humankind or the environment. On the other hand, they have a moral obligation to select work that promotes the social good.[8]

Therein lies the rub—how to go from ethical imperatives to actual practice. Perhaps moral principles are more useful in helping us pose questions than as concrete answers. What is the social value of the problem that a cryptographic system aims to solve? Why are cryptographers really working on a particular problem? Do they aim to satisfy the needs of ordinary people? Do they make good use of their academic freedom? Should they accept military funding? Should they cooperate with government agencies? Are they open to different approaches? Do they attend to what surrounds their field? Do they contribute their knowledge to a cryptographic commons? Do they communicate their findings well?

Such questions can be solved only with discussion, if ever. To come full circle back to where we left off at the end of the preface, if this book has enabled you, the reader, to be part of that discussion, it will have served its purpose.

Figure 68   Figure 69

Figure 70

Figure 71

A last word. Your takeaway should not be a gloomy picture. Cryptography can be thorny, but it has served us well. We enjoy a world of global knowledge, digital communications, and commerce that would simply not exist without modern cryptography. You can see three images in figures 68–70 composed with the aid of *visual cryptography*. They are shares of a secret image. If you take them individually, they show nothing; if you take them in pairs, again they show nothing. But if you put all three of them on top of each other and let light shine through them, you will see the picture in figure 71.[9] Take care.

ACKNOWLEDGMENTS

This book grew out of an idea from Marie Lufkin Lee of the MIT Press, when we were working on my previous book *Algorithms* for the Essential Knowledge series. This volume would not exist without her, and I hope I have done justice to her confidence in me.

Marie retired from the MIT Press as I started writing *Cryptography*, so I had the pleasure of working with Noah J. Springer; my only regret is that I am afraid I may have abused his gentle efforts to keep me on track. My thanks to Cindy Milstein, who copyedited the book, and my gratitude to Virginia Crossman for showing such meticulous care in the final push before publication. Diomidis Spinellis and the anonymous reviewers gave valuable feedback and caught many infelicities; any remaining errors are my fault and my fault only.

Hannah Arendt famously said in her last interview, in 1973, that "there are no dangerous thoughts for the simple reason that thinking itself is such a dangerous enterprise"; that's because "to think always means to think critically. And to think critically is always to be hostile."[1] Perhaps, ensconced in comfortable lives, and taking liberty for granted, we forget how perilous the expression of our thinking can be. This book is for those who, faced with oppression, need to keep their thoughts secret.

Advanced Encryption Standard (AES)
A symmetric cipher standardized by the US National Institute of Standards and Technology (NIST) in 2001. It superseded the older DES.

advertising conversion
The number of people that respond to an advertisement by taking some further action, such as actually clicking on an online ad or buying afterward from a brick-and-mortar store.

associative
A mathematical operation such that for three elements a, b, and c, $a * (b * c) = (a * b) * c$.

asymmetric cryptography
The branch of cryptography that uses one key for the encryption of a message and a different key for its decryption.

authenticate-then-encrypt
Combine AES and MAC by first producing a MAC and then encrypting the plaintext. The CCM mode uses this approach.

authenticity
In cryptography, the property of guaranteeing the integrity of a message.

avalanche effect
A property of a cipher whereby slightly changing the input will result in a significant change in the output.

backdoor
A covert way for bypassing an encryption method.

base (exponentiation)
The number that is raised to a power in the exponentiation operator. In 2^5, the base is 2.

base (lattice)
The vectors that produce the points of the lattice by using addition and multiplication.

base (logarithm)
If $\log_b(x) = y$, b is the base of the logarithm of x. It is the number that will be raised to the exponent y in order to produce the number x—that is, $b^x = y$. For instance, $\log_2(32) = 5$, because the fifth power of the base is equal to 32: $2^5 = 32$.

base (quantum physics)
Two different ways in which a photon can be encoded.

beneficence
The moral principle of working for the benefit of others.

bigram
A sequence of two adjacent letters in a text.

block
A sequence of bytes of a specific length.

block cipher
A cipher that operates by encrypting blocks of plaintext together.

bombe
A machine built in Bletchley Park in World War II, used for the decryption of the German Enigma.

brute force
Solving a problem by trial and error, enumerating all possible solutions until the right one is found. The name reflects that no special intelligence or knowledge is applied to solve the problem.

certificate authority (CA)
A trusted entity that stores, signs, and issues digital certificates.

chain of trust
The chain from one particular certificate authority whose key is signed by another certificate authority, and so on, until we arrive at a root certificate authority.

character encoding
The assignment of numbers to characters so that they can be represented inside a computer.

chord rule
The rule used for the definition of the addition of two points in an elliptic curve.

chosen ciphertext attack (CCA)
A threat model in which the attacker is able to use plaintext and ciphertext pairs for ciphertexts of their choice.

chosen plaintext attack (CPA)
A threat model in which the attacker is able to use plaintext and ciphertext pairs for plaintexts of their choice.

cipher
A method for encrypting a message.

cipher block chaining (CBC) mode
An AES mode in which each block's encryption depends on the previous ciphertext block.

cipher block chaining message authentication code (CBC-MAC)
A MAC constructed by the AES CBC mode.

cipher disk
A polyalphabetic cipher where two alphabets are placed on concentric rotating disks. By rotating the disks, the substitution of a given letter changes.

cipher suite
The set of algorithms used to secure a network communication.

ciphertext
The encrypted message.

ciphertext-only attack (COA)
A threat model in which the attacker only has access to one or more ciphertexts.

cipher wheel
See cipher disk.

circuit
In MPC, a representation of a calculation using simple logical operations called gates.

cleartext
The message that we want to communicate in its original form, before being encrypted.

client
The computer asking for data by requesting it from the server.

closest vector problem (CVP)
The problem of finding the closest lattice point to another point (which may not necessarily be a lattice point). The CVP underlies lattice-based cryptography.

code-based encryption
A branch of PQC.

collision
A collision occurs when a hash function produces the same output for two different inputs. It should be an extremely unlikely occurrence.

commutative
A mathematical operation in which for two elements a and b, $a * b = b * a$.

composite
A composite integer is a positive integer that can be formed by multiplying two other smaller positive integers.

confidentiality
In cryptography, the property of ensuring that only the recipient of a message can have access to its contents.

confusion
A property of a cipher whereby a bit of the ciphertext should depend on several parts of the key, thereby hiding the relationship between the ciphertext and key.

coordinated vulnerability disclosure
The disclosure of a vulnerability to the public once the responsible parties have been notified and given sufficient time to provide a fix.

coprime
Two integers are coprime if their greatest common divisor is 1.

counter (CTR) mode
An AES mode that uses a counter for the encryption of each block. The CTR mode allows us to use AES as a stream cipher.

counter with cipher block chaining message authentication code mode (or simply CCM)
An AES mode that produces a ciphertext and MAC, guaranteeing both confidentiality and authenticity.

crib
A pair of a plaintext and its corresponding ciphertext. Cribs can be important instruments in cryptanalysis.

cryptanalysis
The process of analyzing cryptographic systems in order to understand their functioning. That includes studying their output (ciphertexts) in order to deduce the input (plaintexts).

cryptography
The topic of this book. The study of methods that allow us to communicate securely in the presence of others, who can intercept our communication.

Data Encryption Standard (DES)
A symmetric cipher, developed in the 1970s and superseded by AES.

dead drop
A secret location that is used by spies to exchange messages. One agent drops a message in the dead drop, from where another agent recovers it.

dead letter box
See dead drop. Not to be confused with *Dead Letter Office*, an album by the rock group R.E.M.

Decisional Diffie-Hellman (DDH) assumption
The assumption that for any g^a mod p and g^b mod p, the value g^{ab} mod p is indistinguishable from any random value modulo p. It is a stronger assumption than the one that we cannot solve the discrete logarithm problem and the basis of numerous modern cryptographic constructions.

decryption
The process that reverses the effects of encryption and turns the ciphertext back into the plaintext.

degree (of a polynomial)
In polynomials of one variable, the largest power of the variable that appears in a term of the polynomial. The polynomial $3x^2 - 2x + 1$ is of degree 2. In polynomials with more than one variable, the degree is the highest sum of the powers in the terms. The polynomial $3x^2y^3 + 4x - 9$ is of degree 5.

differential cryptanalysis
A form of cryptanalysis in which we study how differences in the input of a cryptographic method affect its output.

Diffie-Hellman key exchange
A method for exchanging keys based on the discrete logarithm problem, published by Whitfield Diffie and Martin Hellman in 1976. The method solved the key distribution problem, as it allows two parties to agree on a shared secret key even though all of their communication happens over a public channel.

diffusion
A property of a cipher whereby changing a bit of the plaintext should change half the bits of the ciphertext, thus diffusing the effect of the change throughout the encryption output.

digital certificate
A digital document that verifies the validity of a public key. More generally, a digital attestation for something.

digital fingerprint
A short digital sequence that identifies a digital document, typically produced by a one-way hash function.

digital signature
A digital mark, provided through a cryptographic method, that binds a document with its author, verifying its authenticity.

discrete logarithm problem
The problem of finding the logarithm of modular exponentiation. If we have $g^x \bmod p$, find x, given p and g. We do not know an efficient way to do that. The discrete logarithm problem underlies many modern cryptographic systems.

eavesdropper
A person, usually called Eve, who is able to intercept the communication between two or more parties.

electronic code book (ECB) mode
The basic AES mode of operation, corresponding to bare-bones AES.

ElGamal encryption
An encryption system, described by Taher Elgamal in 1985, based on the discrete logarithm problem. It uses the Diffie-Hellman key exchange to establish a secret that encrypts the message.

elliptic curve
In real numbers, an elliptic curve is a curve in the plane defined by an equation of the form $y^2 = x^3 + ax + b$, where a and b are real numbers. Elliptic curves have no sharp corners, called cusps, or intersections, called nodes.

elliptic curve cryptography (ECC)
Public key cryptography based on elliptic curves.

elliptic curve discrete logarithm problem
The equivalent of the discrete logarithm problem when dealing with elliptic curves.

encryption
The process of turning a message into one that is unintelligible to anybody except its intended recipient.

encrypt-then-authenticate
Combines AES and MAC by first encrypting the ciphertext and then producing a MAC. The GCM mode uses this approach.

exponent
The power in the exponentiation operation.

exponentiation operation
Raising a number, called the base, to a power, called the exponent. That is, multiplying the base repeatedly by the number of times indicated by the exponent. It is symbolized by x^y. For example, $2^5 = 2 \times 2 \times 2 \times 2 \times 2 = 32$.

extended Euclidean algorithm
An extension of the Euclidean algorithm. The Euclidean algorithm is an algorithm for computing the greatest common divisor between two numbers. The extended Euclidean algorithm, given two integers a, b, computes two integers x and y such that $ax + by = gcd(a, b)$. If $gcd(a, b) = 1$, the number x is the modular multiplicative inverse of a modulo b.

factorial
The factorial of an integer is the product of all positive integers less than or equal to that integer. For example, $5! = 5 \times 4 \times 3 \times 2 \times 1 = 120$.

factorization
The decomposition of an integer number into a product of integers, which are its prime factors.

frequency analysis
The analysis of the frequencies of symbols or groups of symbols that appear in an encrypted message in order to find the encryption key.

fundamental theorem of arithmetic
The theorem in arithmetic according to which any integer greater than 1 can be written as a unique product of prime numbers, which are called its prime factors.

Galois / counter mode (GCM)
An AES mode that operates in the encrypt-then-authenticate manner.

garbling
A technique used in MPC protocols to encrypt circuits.

gate
In a circuit, a simple logical operation. For instance, an AND gate takes two inputs that may be true or false and outputs true when both of the inputs are true. The OR gate takes two inputs that may be true or false and outputs true when either of them is true.

general MPC protocol
A cryptographic protocol that can be used to compute any function.

greatest common divisor (GCD)
For two or more nonzero integer numbers, the greatest common divisor is the largest positive integer that divides each one of them.

hash algorithm
The algorithm that is implemented by a hash function.

hash-based cryptography
A branch of PQC.

hash function
A one-way function that takes as input a digital document and outputs a short digital sequence (the digital digest) that identifies the document. A hash function should produce message digests with a low probability of collisions.

heuristic security
The analysis of the security of a cryptographic system based on practical approaches that rely on informal strategies, like trial and error as well as rules learned from experience.

homomorphic encryption
Encryption methods that allow us to perform mathematical operations on the encrypted data, which when decrypted will be equivalent to having performed the operations on their plaintexts.

host
A computer hosting a network service.

hybrid encryption
Encryption that combines symmetric and public key cryptography. Typically, public key cryptography is used to create a shared secret key that is then used with symmetric cryptography.

hypertext transfer protocol (HTTP)
The request-response protocol that is used for the exchange of messages between browsers and servers on the World Wide Web.

hypertext transfer protocol secure (HTTPS)
The HTTP protocol used along with TLS to offer secure browsing on the web.

identity element
In a mathematical operation, an element such that the result of the operation of any element with the identity element is the original element. In addition, the identity element is 0. In multiplication, the identity element is 1.

incident
A breach of security in a system.

initialization vector
In cryptography, a sequence of bits used to initialize a cryptographic method.

integer prime factorization
See factorization.

intermediate certificate authority
A certificate authority that is not directly trusted by the browser, but whose key is signed by another certificate authority, whose key is in turn signed by another certificate authority, and so on, thus creating a chain of trust up to a root certificate authority.

inverse
In a mathematical operation, given an element a, the element that when combined with a produces the identity element. In addition, the inverse of a is $-a$. In multiplication, it is the reciprocal $1/a$.

key
The piece of knowledge that the recipient of an encrypted message must possess in order to decrypt it.

key distribution problem
The problem of distributing to the parties of a communication the secret key that can decrypt the ciphertexts in the communication.

known-plaintext attack (KPA)
A threat model in which the attacker has access to a set of pairs of known plaintexts and their corresponding ciphertexts.

Lagrangian interpolation
A mathematical method to find a polynomial that passes through a specific set of points.

lattice
A set of points in a multidimensional space that forms a crystalline structure. If we add or subtract two points in a lattice, we get another point on the lattice. Two lattice points cannot be closer than some minimum distance, and every point is no further away than some maximum distance from a lattice point.

lattice-based encryption
A branch of PQC.

logarithm operation
The inverse of the exponentiation operation. If $x^n = y$, $\log_y x = n$. The number y is the base of the logarithm. The logarithm of a number gives us the exponent that we have to use for a given base to obtain the number.

malleable
A cryptographic method in which it is possible for an attacker to transform a ciphertext to another ciphertext that decrypts to a plaintext related to the plaintext of the original ciphertext.

malware
Software that is intentionally designed to cause harm.

message authentication code (MAC)
A short piece of information that verifies the integrity of a message and guarantees that it corresponds to a specific plaintext.

message digest
See digital fingerprint.

mode of operation
In AES, a specific setup consisting of the basic AES construction along with additional modules that offers increased features, such as better security guarantees, or allows AES to operate as a stream cipher.

modular arithmetic
Arithmetic using integer numbers, where the result of operations are "wrapped around" when they reach a certain value, called the modulus. Time arithmetic is modular; when minutes reach sixty, they wrap around and start again from zero.

modular exponentiation
The exponentiation operation in modular arithmetic. It is equal to raising a base to the exponent and then taking the remainder of the division with a modulus. An essential part of cryptographic algorithms.

modular multiplicative inverse
The inverse of a number in modular arithmetic. As in ordinary arithmetic, when we multiply a number with its inverse we get 1. In contrast to ordinary arithmetic, a number does not always have a modular multiplicative inverse and the modular multiplicative inverse of a number a is not the reciprocal $1/a$. For example, the modular multiplicative inverse of 3 modulo 40 is 27, because $3 \cdot 27 \bmod 40 = 81 \bmod 40 = 1$. If a number has a modular multiplicative inverse, we can find it with the extended Euclidean algorithm. A number has a modular multiplicative inverse if the greatest common divisor of the number and the modulus is 1—that is, they are relative prime or coprimes.

modulo
The remainder of a division. For example, 5 mod 2 equals 1.

modulus
In modular arithmetic, the threshold where integers wrap around. In time arithmetic, which is modular, the modulus is sixty.

monoalphabetic cipher
A substitution cipher that always replaces a given letter with the same corresponding letter.

n-gram
A sequence of a number of adjacent letters, usually more than two when we have a bigram.

nonce
In cryptography, a value that is produced in order to be used only once during encryption.

nonmaleficence
The moral principle of inflicting no harm to others.

number theory
The branch of mathematics devoted to the study of integers and arithmetic functions.

oblivious transfer
A cryptographic technique in which a sender sends one among different possible values to a recipient, but remains oblivious as to which value they have sent.

one-time pad
An unbreakable cryptographic method where each letter of a message is substituted with another letter, given by a sequence of random letters (the key) that must be at least as long as the message.

1–2 oblivious transfer
Oblivious transfer in which one party, Alice, sends to another party, Bob, one out of two possible values, with Alice remaining oblivious as to which value she has actually sent to Bob.

one-way function
A function that can easily compute a result given some input, but whose result is difficult to reverse and go back to the input.

open-source
Software whose source code is openly available to the public, allowing anyone to inspect, copy, modify, and redistribute it.

optimal asymmetric encryption padding (OAEP), or RSA-OAEP
A padding scheme used with RSA.

padding
In computer science, the practice of filling up space with additional data. In RSA, we take the plaintext and random data and combine them up to the size of the modulus before encryption, in order to make RSA nondeterministic and increase security.

PKCS #1 (Public Key Cryptography Standard #1)
A standard (the first in a series) published by RSA Laboratories, a security company founded by the inventors of RSA.

plaintext
See cleartext.

point at infinity
The identity element in elliptic curves.

polyalphabetic cipher
A substitution cipher that uses different substitutions for a given letter at different parts of the message.

polynomial
A mathematical expression that is built from a sum of terms, where each term is the product of variables, each of which can be raised to integer powers, and a constant number, called a coefficient. For example, $3x^2 - 2x + 1$ is a polynomial with terms $3x^2$, $-2x$, and 1. The numbers 3, -2, and 1 are the coefficients of the polynomial.

post-quantum cryptography (PQC)
Cryptographic methods that are immune from advances in quantum computing and therefore secure even when (if) powerful quantum computers become a reality.

prime
An integer is a prime if it is greater than 1 and is not the product of two smaller natural numbers. In other words, it can be divided only by 1 and itself. An integer greater than 1 that is not a prime is a composite. The number 1 is neither a prime nor a composite.

prime factors
For a given integer greater than 1, the prime numbers that, when multiplied together, produce the number.

private key
In public key cryptography, the part of the key pair that is private.

private set intersection problem
The problem where two parties can compare two encrypted sets in order to find their intersection, without having to decrypt the sets.

provable security
The analysis of the security of a cryptographic system based on rigorous mathematical proofs.

pseudorandom
A number that appears to be random, but is in fact generated by a pseudorandom number generator.

pseudorandom number generator
An algorithm that produces a sequence of numbers that appear to be random, even though in fact they are produced deterministically.

public key
In public key cryptography, the part of the key pair that is public.

public key cryptography
The field of cryptography that uses pairs of cryptographic keys, one of them private and the other public.

quantum algorithm
An algorithm that harnesses quantum properties for its operation.

quantum bit (qubit)
The basic unit of information in quantum computing.

quantum computing
Methods that harness the properties of quantum physics to build more powerful computers.

quantum cryptography
Cryptography that uses the properties of quantum physics.

quantum key distribution (QKD)
A key exchange method that uses the properties of quantum physics.

ransomware
A kind of malware that uses cryptography to lock users out of their data until a ransom is paid.

real-world security
The security of a cryptographic system out in the wild.

reduction
The reduction of one hard computational problem to another. If we reduce problem X to problem Y, then if we find an efficient method to solve X, with little extra effort we will be able to solve Y as well.

relative prime
See coprime.

request
A message sent by a computer (the client) asking for some data from another computer (the server).

response
A message sent by a computer (the server) responding to a request for some data by another computer (the client).

responsible disclosure
See coordinated vulnerability disclosure.

root certificate authority
A certificate authority that is trusted by the web browsers. Root certificate authorities must meet specific technical requirements, so the corresponding barriers of entry mean that there is a limited number of them.

round
In a cryptographic method, one iteration of encryption operations.

router
A networking device that forwards packets of data between computer networks.

RSA
RSA (named after its inventors, Rivest-Shamir-Adleman) is one of the oldest public key cryptographic systems, published in 1977. With the Diffie-Hellman key exchange, it revolutionized cryptography, solving the key distribution problem and ushering in asymmetric cryptography.

salt
In cryptography, random data that is used as additional input to a one-way function.

scheme (URL)
The first part of a URL, such as HTTP or HTTPS, specifying the kind of communication that will be launched.

secret sharing
A cryptographic protocol that is used when we want to share a secret among different parties so that the secret can be revealed only when a specified number of shares are combined and no information can be revealed about the secret with any smaller number of shares.

secure multiparty communication (secure MPC)
The field of cryptography studying methods that enable different parties to compute a function together based on the input of each individual party while keeping these inputs private.

security engineering
The discipline of building systems that are robust against malice, error, or just bad luck. Security engineering uses cryptography, but also encompasses a wider spectrum of tools and methods to design, implement, and operate a system with security requirements in the real world.

self-reciprocal
An encryption method where, to decrypt the message, we pass it through the same process that was used for encryption. In other words, to obtain the plaintext, we feed the ciphertext to the encryption method.

sequential search
Looking for an item among a group of items by examining each one of them in turn.

server
The computer providing the data requested by a client.

Shor's algorithm
A quantum algorithm for integer factorization—that is, for finding the prime factors of an integer—developed in 1994 by Peter Shor.

side-channel attack
In computer security, an attack that uses extra information that can be gleaned from the operation or implementation of the system rather than from flaws that can be found by studying the design of the underlying cryptographic methods themselves or the corresponding computer code.

social engineering
In information security, an attack that dupes people to achieve the desired outcome, such as revealing confidential information (for instance, passwords) or performing specific actions (like transferring money to an adversary's account).

state (AES)
In AES, the ciphertext through the various stages and rounds of the encryption process.

store-now-decrypt-later
Storing encrypted messages now with a view toward decrypting them in the future, when advances in quantum computing will have broken the encryption method.

stream cipher
A cipher that works by transforming each digit of the plaintext at a time to a ciphertext. Contrast with block cipher.

substitution cipher
A cipher that works by substituting a letter of the alphabet with another one or in general a symbol with another symbol (because a message may contain not just letters but also digits, etc.).

superposition
The property of quantum physics that allows a qubit to exist in two states, 0 and 1, simultaneously.

supersingular elliptic curve isogeny
A branch of PQC.

symmetric cryptography
The branch of cryptography that uses the same key for the encryption and decryption of a message.

symmetric encryption
See symmetric cryptography.

tag
In cryptography, a MAC.

tangent rule
The rule used for the definition of the multiplication of an integer with a point in an elliptic curve.

threat model
A model that describes a particular kind of attack on a cryptographic system. A threat model depicts the capabilities of the attacker and the means that the adversary can use to mount an attack.

TLS handshake
The initials steps of the TLS protocol where the client and server agree on the cryptographic methods and keys they will use in their session.

TLS record
The packets that carry encrypted data in TLS.

TLS record protocol
A protocol that describes TLS records.

TLS session
A communication between a client and server using the TLS protocol.

transport layer security (TLS)
A cryptographic protocol that provides secure communication over a computer network.

Turing machine
A model of computation proposed by Alan Turing. The Turing machine describes an abstract machine that manipulates symbols on a table, based on a table of rules. Despite its simplicity, it is capable of implementing any computer algorithm.

uniform resource locator (URL)
A technical term for an address on the World Wide Web.

vector
A mathematical object that cannot be expressed by a single number. In two dimensions, a vector is a segment that has a magnitude and direction.

visual cryptography
Cryptographic method that allows visual information, such as pictures, to be encrypted, so that the ciphertext and corresponding plaintext are visual images.

vulnerability
A security weakness in a system.

window of vulnerability
The interval between the time when a vulnerability is discovered and a fix for it is found.

zero-day vulnerability
Vulnerabilities that are unknown to those who would be responsible for fixing them, like the makers of a software application or providers of a service.

zeroth term (of a polynomial)
The term with zeroth power. In the polynomial $3x^2 - 2x + 1$, it is the term 1.

NOTES

Chapter 1

1. The book has been translated in other languages, where the translators have followed the restriction on dispensing with the most frequent letter. In English, it has been translated as *A Void* by Gilbert Adair (1995). Here is an excerpt from the text: "A gap will yawn, achingly, day by day, it will turn into a colossal pit, an abyss without foundation, a gradual invasion of words by margins, blank and insignificant, so that all of us, to a man, will find nothing to say."

2. Mayzner and Tresselt, "Tables of Single-Letter and Digram Frequency Counts for Various Word-Length and Letter-Position Combinations."

3. The quote comes from Lieberman et al., "Quantifying the Evolutionary Dynamics of Language," an excellent study of the evolution of human language.

4. For a readable, best-selling introduction to cryptography with a fast-paced historical account, see Singh, *The Code Book*. For a comprehensive history of cryptography up to the 1960s, see Kahn, *The Codebreakers*. Our historical synopsis owes a lot to it. For a book mixing cryptographic history with details on cryptographic principles and cryptanalysis, see Bauer, *Decrypted Secrets*.

5. The source for this image is Yrithinnd, Wikimedia Commons, February 16, 2007, https://commons.wikimedia.org/w/index.php?curid=23821, available under a CC BY-SA 3.0 license.

6. For an examination of the references of scytale in antiquity, questioning whether it was actually used by the Spartans to hide their messages, see Kelly, "The Myth of the Skytale."

7. Suetonius, *De Vita XII Caesarum*, Divus Julius, 56.6, published in the Loeb Classical Library series (1913); text is in the public domain.

8. Here is why. Remember the definition of integer division: if we have two integers a and b, the division of a by b gives us two integers, the quotient q and the remainder r, with $0 \leq r < b$, such that $a = q \times b + r$ (if the division is exact, $r = 0$). Therefore, the remainder is $r = a - q \times b$. The quotient is the greatest integer less than or equal to the fraction a/b. If we have $a = -4$ and $b = 26$, the quotient is $q = -4/26 = -1$ and the remainder is $r = -4 - (-1) \times 26 = -4 + 26 = 22$.

9. The quotation is from Al-Kadi, "Origins of Cryptology."

10. According to Ibrahim Al-Kadi ("Origins of Cryptology"), "The concept of the *zero* or *sifr* or *cipher* was so confusing and ambiguous to common Europeans at first that a person used to say in arguments or discussions that he

is 'talking about something clear and comprehensible, and not about some ambiguous and far-fetched thing like the cipher.'"

11. Quinn DuPont ("The Printing Press and Cryptography") argues that Alberti may have been influenced in his development of the cipher disk by the invention of movable type by Johannes Gutenberg.

12. Bellovin, "Frank Miller."

13. John von Neumann made the remark at a conference in 1949. The conference papers were published in 1951; see von Neumann, "Various Techniques Used in Connection with Random Digits," 36.

14. The photograph of Enigma was taken by Alessandro Nassiri, and the source is Museo della Scienza e della Tecnologia, "Leonardo da Vinci," posted by OS, Wikimedia Commons, April 20, 2016, https://commons.wikimedia.org/w/index.php?curid=47910919, available under a CC BY-SA 4.0 license.

15. There were various versions of the Enigma machine. Here we describe the version used by the army and air force. The version used by the navy was more secure, but the underlying design was the same. Also, in our description we omit part of the mechanism called "ring setting," as it does not change the basic idea of its operation.

16. "There is no *minimum length* of an enciphered message; *maximum* length is 250 letters." Paragraph 126 of the Enigma instruction manual, translated at Bletchley Park, transcribed and formatted by Tony Sale, available at https://www.codesandciphers.org.uk/documents/egenproc/egenproc.pdf. Sale was a British electronics, software, and hardware engineer as well as a historian of computing. This manual, published in 1940, was for the navy version of Enigma. Different versions had different length limits. "The limit for the Army ENIGMA was 180 characters, increased to 250 characters after Jan. 13, 1940, 320 characters for the navy Enigma." Bauer, *Decrypted Secrets*, 217.

17. For an analysis of the mathematics behind Enigma, see Miller, "The Cryptographic Mathematics of Enigma."

18. A popular explanation for the term "bombe" is that it was named after an ice cream bombe. Enigma was first analyzed by a group of Polish cryptologists, who initially designed a machine for the decryption efforts. The idea for the machine came while they were eating an ice cream bombe, so one of them, Jerzy Różycki, named the machine *bomba* in Polish. The story comes from the commander of the group, Tadeusz Lisicki. There are also other explanations, but they are more prosaic. See Link, "Resurrecting Bomba Kryptologiczna."

19. This is necessarily a summary exposition of Enigma and its deciphering. For a readable exposition, from where the crib example was taken, see Singh, *The Code Book*. For a description of the operational weaknesses and human

errors that were instrumental to the breaking of Enigma, see Ratcliff, "How Statistics Led the Germans to Believe Enigma Secure and Why They Were Wrong."

Chapter 2

1. Dickens, *The Posthumous Papers of the Pickwick Club,* 694, 700.

2. For Dickens and advertising, see Schlicke, *Oxford Reader's Companion to Dickens*; Horn, "Dickens and the Patent Bramah Lock"; Williams, "Advertising and Fiction in the *Pickwick Papers.*"

3. The Challenge Lock is in the Science Museum in London. The source of this photograph is Geni, Wikimedia Commons, June 17, 2022, https://commons .wikimedia.org/w/index.php?curid=119396870, available under a CC BY-SA 4.0 license.

4. For an account of the breaking of the Challenge Lock, see Kastner, "A. C. Hobbs and the Great Lock Controversy of 1851." The news item appeared in the September 6, 1851, issue of the *Economist* (vol. 9, no. 419, 986) under News of the Week. Like the *Economist,* the Bramah lock company is still in business in London. Two hundred guineas was equivalent to £210, which is £26,210 (or about $33,082) in February 2024, according to the Bank of England inflation calculator, at https://www.bankofengland.co.uk/monetary -policy/inflation/inflation-calculator, and using the average exchange rate of pounds to dollars for that month.

5. Churchill, "The Spectacle of Security."

6. Bramah's "A Dissertation on the Construction of Locks," is available at https://books.google.gr/books?id=EGcFAAAAQAAJ. His petition to the House of Commons is available at https://books.google.gr/books?id=CjtcAA AAcAAJ.

7. Hobbs, *Locks and Safes,* 3.

8. See Kerckhoffs, "La Cryptographie Militaire, Première Partie"; Kerckhoffs, "La Cryptographie Militaire, Seconde Partie." For the six principles (or desiderata as he called them), see Kerckhoffs, "La Cryptographie Militaire, Première Partie," 12. For Kerckhoffs's explanation of secrecy, see Kerckhoffs, "La Cryptographie Militaire, Première Partie," 14.

9. National Institute of Standards and Technology (NIST), "Announcing Development of a Federal Information Processing Standard for Advanced Encryption Standard."

10. See the DESCHALL press release of June 18, 1997, archived at https:// web.archive.org/web/20071201071615/http://home.earthlink.net/~rcv007 /despr4.htm.

11. For the announcement of AES, see National Institute of Standards and Technology (NIST), "Announcing the ADVANCED ENCRYPTION STANDARD (AES)." For an in-depth description by its creators, see Daemen and Rijmen, *The Design of Rijndael*.

12. Shannon's classified report was *A Mathematical Theory of Cryptography*, memorandum MM 45-110-02, September 1, 1945, Bell Laboratories. For the declassified version, see Shannon, "Communication Theory of Secrecy Systems."

13. Hardy, *A Mathematician's Apology*, 121–122.

14. The strict avalanche criterion was introduced in Webster and Tavares, "On the Design of S-Boxes."

15. The source of the 1200 × 1260 pixel version of this image is Otto Messmer, converted to vector by Tom Edwards, and posted by GaryBarbaree, Wikimedia Commons, January 30, 2019, https://commons.wikimedia.org/wiki/File:Felix_the_Cat.jpg. It is in the public domain.

Chapter 3

1. According to Ed Glinert (*The London Compendium*, 421), "During the 1980s the KGB had a dead letter box (a safe place where they could leave secret documents and messages) in a recess behind a column by the altar." More precisely, the altar is on the right of the entrance and has a copy of Michelangelo's *Pietà* statue. To the left of the altar are two large marble columns; the dead letter box was between the column nearest the wall and the wall. For the history behind this (its location was leaked by a double agent), see Berkeley, *A Spy's London*.

2. The paint analogy comes from Singh, *The Code Book*.

3. Diffie and Hellman, "New Directions in Cryptography."

4. See Elgamal, "A Public Key Cryptosystem and a Signature Scheme Based on Discrete Logarithms."

5. "The Decision Diffie-Hellman assumption (DDH) is a gold mine. It enables one to construct efficient cryptographic systems with strong security properties." Boneh, "The Decision Diffie-Hellman Problem." The rest of the paper explores several applications of DDH, including ElGamal.

6. In cryptography, we may run out of mathematical symbols. In research papers, to avoid confusion, cryptographers use different fonts like Fraktur. 𝔗𝔢𝔵𝔱 𝔦𝔫 𝔉𝔯𝔞𝔨𝔱𝔲𝔯 𝔩𝔬𝔬𝔨𝔰 𝔩𝔦𝔨𝔢 𝔱𝔥𝔦𝔰.

7. Rivest, Shamir, and Adleman, "A Method for Obtaining Digital Signatures and Public-Key Cryptosystems."

8. The example is a modified version of the one given in Rivest, Shamir, and Adleman, "A Method for Obtaining Digital Signatures and Public-Key

Cryptosystems." The phrase is from William Shakespeare's *Julius Caesar*, act 1, scene 2, line 283, in the Arden Shakespeare Third Series edition.

9. See the Cramer-Shoup cryptosystem (Cramer and Shoup, "A Practical Public Key Cryptosystem Provably Secure against Adaptive Chosen Ciphertext Attack") and Diffie-Hellman integrated encryption scheme (Abdalla, Bellare, and Rogaway, "The Oracle Diffie-Hellman Assumptions and an Analysis of DHIES").

10. Moriarty et al., "PKCS #1: RSA Cryptography Specifications Version 2.2."

11. See Adrian et al., "Imperfect Forward Secrecy," which ends, "A key lesson from this state of affairs is that cryptographers and creators of practical systems need to work together more effectively. System builders should take responsibility for being aware of applicable cryptanalytic attacks. Cryptographers, for their part, should involve themselves in how crypto is actually being applied, such as through engagement with standards efforts and software review. Bridging the perilous gap that separates these communities will be essential for keeping future systems secure" (16).

12. The SHA-2 standard was announced in National Institute of Standards and Technology (NIST), "Announcing Development of Federal Information Processing Standard (FIPS) 180-2, Secure Hash Standard; a Revision of FIPS 180-1." It was updated in National Institute of Standards and Technology (NIST), "Announcing Development of Federal Information Processing Standard (FIPS) 180-4, Secure Hash Standard (SHS); a Revision of FIPS 180-3."

Chapter 4

1. This image, available at https://upload.wikimedia.org/wikipedia/commons /1/13/First_Internet_Demonstration%2C_1977.jpg, comes from the Computer History Museum and is in the public domain.

2. Rescorla, "The Transport Layer Security (TLS) Protocol Version 1.3."

3. Shamir, "How to Share a Secret."

4. The curves here are based on the methods described in Bruggeman and Gush, "Nice Cubic Polynomials for Curve Sketching"; Evard, "Polynomials Whose Roots and Critical Points Are Integers." They have integer roots and integer inflection points, and are convenient for illustration purposes—but we cannot use them for actual secret sharing, as we explain later on.

5. For an overview, see Lindell, "Secure Multiparty Computation."

6. For a description of the Estonian student and taxes application, see Bogdanov et al., "Students and Taxes." For the Boston wage study, see Lapets et al., "Accessible Privacy-Preserving Web-Based Data Analysis for Assessing and Addressing Economic Inequalities." For the way Google solved the ad conversion

rate problem, see Ion et al., "Private Intersection-Sum Protocol with Applications to Attributing Aggregate Ad Conversions."

7. For an example employing private set intersection on the human genome, see Baldi et al., "Countering GATTACA." For descriptions of fast private set intersection protocols with better properties than the naive protocol that we outline here, see Pinkas, Schneider, and Zohner, "Scalable Private Set Intersection Based on OT Extension"; Pinkas et al., "SpOT-Light."

8. Du and Atallah, "Protocols for Secure Remote Database Access with Approximate Matching."

9. Oblivious transfer was introduced in Rabin, "How to Exchange Secrets with Oblivious Transfer." And 1–2 oblivious transfer was developed in Even, Goldreich, and Lempel, "A Randomized Protocol for Signing Contracts."

Chapter 5

1. ECC was introduced independently in Koblitz, "Elliptic Curve Cryptosystems"; Miller, "Use of Elliptic Curves in Cryptography." For cryptographic applications of elliptic curves, see Blake, Seroussi, and Smart, *Elliptic Curves in Cryptography*; Blake, Seroussi, and Smart, *Advances in Elliptic Curve Cryptography*; Hankerson, Menezes, and Vanstone, *Guide to Elliptic Curve Cryptography*. For a detailed exposition, including the mathematical underpinnings, see Washington, *Elliptic Curves*.

2. This is the crypto-incarnation of David Hume's "is-ought problem," as he pointed out in *A Treatise of Human Nature* (1739): "In every system of morality, which I have hitherto met with, I have always remarked, that the author proceeds for some time in the ordinary way of reasoning, and establishes the being of a God, or makes observations concerning human affairs; when of a sudden I am surprised to find, that instead of the usual copulations of propositions, *is*, and *is not*, I meet with no proposition that is not connected with an *ought*, or an *ought not*."

3. The estimates are from table 2 in Barker, "Recommendation for Key Management."

4. Worries about the security of an NSA-proposed ECC standard were raised in 2005. In 2013, "the New York Times, the Guardian and ProPublica reported the existence of a secret National Security Agency SIGINT Enabling Project with the mission to 'actively [engage] the US and foreign IT industries to covertly influence and/or overtly leverage their commercial products' designs.'" Checkoway et al., "On the Practical Exploitability of Dual EC in TLS Implementations," 319. The SafeCurves project (http://safecurves.cr.yp.to/), run

by leading cryptographers, aims at "choosing safe curves for elliptic-curve cryptography."

5. The lectures were published the following year and have since been reprinted in Feynman, *The Character of Physical Law*; the quote is on page 129.

6. At the same time, apart from Feynman, Russian mathematician Yuri Manin and US physicist Paul Benioff also proposed, each of them independently of the other two, harnessing quantum physics for computing purposes. See Preskill, "Quantum Computing 40 Years Later."

7. The QKD protocol we described is the BB84 protocol, named after its inventors, Charles H. Bennett and Gilles Brassard, and the year of its publication. See Bennett and Brassard, "Quantum Cryptography." For the practical problems of QKD, see Scarani and Kurtsiefer, "The Black Paper of Quantum Cryptography."

8. For Shor's algorithm, see Shor, "Algorithms for Quantum Computation"; Shor, "Polynomial-Time Algorithms for Prime Factorization and Discrete Logarithms on a Quantum Computer." For Grover's algorithm, see Grover, "A Fast Quantum Mechanical Algorithm for Database Search." For a two-page visual introduction to quantum computing, which also inspired our illustrations, see Trabesinger, "Quantum Leaps, Bit by Bit." For introductions to quantum computing, see Rieffel and Polak, *Quantum Computing*; Lipton and Regan, *Introduction to Quantum Algorithms via Linear Algebra*; Aaronson, *Quantum Computing since Democritus*; Nielsen and Chuang, *Quantum Computation and Quantum Information*.

9. For an overview of PQC, see Bernstein and Lange, "Post-Quantum Cryptography." For the organizational challenges of transitioning to PQC, see Joseph et al., "Transitioning Organizations to Post-Quantum Cryptography."

10. The figure is based on Bill Tourloupis's example at https://texample.net/tikz/examples/lattice-points/.

11. The attack is described in Castryck and Decru, "An Efficient Key Recovery Attack on SIDH (Preliminary Version)."

12. The story is recounted in detail in Kahn, *The Codebreakers*, and in condensed form in Katz and Lindell, *Introduction to Modern Cryptography*.

13. The opening salvo was Koblitz, "The Uneasy Relationship between Mathematics and Cryptography." The snobbery letter is Krawczyk, "Koblitz's Arguments Disingenuous." The slander letter is Wigderson, "Brief History of the Foundations of Cryptography."

14. See Damgård, "A 'Proof-Reading' of Some Issues in Cryptography"; Koblitz and Menezes, "The Brave New World of Bodacious Assumptions in Cryptography."

15. For power analyses against Diffie-Helmann and RSA, see Kocher, "Timing Attacks on Implementations of Diffie-Hellman, RSA, DSS, and Other Systems"; Kocher, Jaffe, and Jun, "Differential Power Analysis."

16. The author does not indulge.

17. For a comprehensive treatment by one of the most prominent people in the field, see Anderson, *Security Engineering*.

Epilogue

1. You can find more details on the scandal in "2022 Greek Surveillance Scandal," Wikipedia, last edited March 29, 2024, https://en.wikipedia.org/wiki/2022_Greek_wiretapping_scandal.

2. Steven Pinker (*The Better Angels of Our Nature*) makes the argument that violence across the world has declined massively in history thanks to the emergence of nation-states as the holders of monopolies of force.

3. This is in the *Republic*, bk 3, sec. 403e, in Paul Shorey's translation. The *Republic* has been harshly criticized for being a brilliant advocacy for authoritarianism: the city described in the *Republic* is not a democratic polity, and indeed Plato was concerned with how to create a political system that would prevent what he saw as the abuses and dangers of democracy. The totalitarian streak in the *Republic* has been analyzed by, among others, Austrian philosopher Karl Popper in *The Open Society and Its Enemies*, written in 1945.

4. For an account of how fear has been used to shape human affairs, see Peckam, *Fear*.

5. Newton was particularly concerned that the Christian doctrine had been polluted over the years and "believed that he had been chosen by God to discover the truth about the decline of Christianity, and he believed it to be by far the most important work he would ever undertake." Iliffe, *Newton*, 72.

6. For ransomware in general, see "Ransomware," Wikipedia, last edited March 27, 2024, https://en.wikipedia.org/wiki/Ransomware. For the attack on the Health Service Executive, see "Health Service Executive Ransomware Attack," Wikipedia, last edited March 22, 2024, https://en.wikipedia.org/wiki/Health_Service_Executive_ransomware_attack.

7. For the original paper introducing ransomware in 1996, see Young and Yung, "Cryptovirology: Extortion-Based Security Threats and Countermeasures." For the June 2017 follow-up, see Young and Yung, "Cryptovirology: The Birth, Neglect, and Explosion of Ransomware."

8. The moral imperative to do no harm is called *nonmaleficence*, while the obligation to work for the benefit of others is called *beneficence*. See Beauchamp and Childress, *Principles of Biomedical Ethics*. The two terms are equivalent to

the positive and negative rights defined in Rogaway, "The Moral Character of Cryptographic Work," from which we have adapted the list of questions in the following paragraph. For the moral issues raised by the cooperation of cryptographers with government agencies, see Regalado, "Cryptographers Have an Ethics Problem"; Bohannon, "Breach of Trust." Regarding the environment, cryptocurrencies have received considerable flak for their amount of carbon emissions—and cryptographers have come up with approaches to solve the problem.

9. See Naor and Shamir, "Visual Cryptography." The source of the laughing smiley image is Pd4u, Wikimedia Commons, August 2017, https://commons .wikimedia.org/wiki/File:Laughing-smiley.svg. It is in the public domain. If you really want to experiment with the images, you should enlarge them because their resolution is probably too low on this printed page. Alternatively, you can put them one on top of the other digitally. Or you can trust the author, but what has trust to do with cryptography?

Acknowledgments

1. Roger Errera, "Interviewing Hannah Arendt," HannahArendt.Net, October 1973, https://doi.org/10.57773/hanet.v2i1.190.

BIBLIOGRAPHY

Aaronson, Scott. *Quantum Computing since Democritus*. Cambridge: Cambridge University Press, 2013.

Abdalla, Michel, Mihir Bellare, and Phillip Rogaway. "The Oracle Diffie-Hellman Assumptions and an Analysis of DHIES." In *Topics in Cryptology—CT-RSA 2001*, edited by David Naccache, 143–158. Berlin: Springer-Verlag, 2001.

Adrian, David, Karthikeyan Bhargavan, Zakir Durumeric, Pierrick Gaudry, Matthew Green, J. Alex Halderman, Nadia Heninger, et al. "Imperfect Forward Secrecy: How Diffie-Hellman Fails in Practice." In *Proceedings of the 22nd ACM SIGSAC Conference on Computer and Communications Security*, 5–17. New York: Association for Computing Machinery, 2015. https://doi.org/10.1145 /2810103.2813707.

Al-Kadi, Ibrahim A. "Origins of Cryptology: The Arab Contributions." *Cryptologia* 16, no. 2 (1992): 97–127.

Anderson, Ross. *Security Engineering: A Guide to Building Dependable Distributed Systems*. 3rd ed. Indianapolis: John Wiley and Sons, 2020.

Baldi, Pierre, Roberta Baronio, Emiliano De Cristofaro, Paolo Gasti, and Gene Tsudik. "Countering GATTACA: Efficient and Secure Testing of Fully-Sequenced Human Genomes." In *Proceedings of the 18th ACM Conference on Computer and Communications Security*, 691–702. New York: Association for Computing Machinery, 2011. https://doi.org/10.1145/2046707.2046785.

Barker, Elaine. "Recommendation for Key Management: Part 1—General." In *NIST Special Publication 800–57 Part 1, Revision 5*. Gaithersburg, MD: National Institute of Standards and Technology, 2020. https://doi.org/10.6028/NIST .SP.800-57pt1r5.

Bauer, Friedrich L. *Decrypted Secrets: Methods and Maxims of Cryptology*. 4th ed. Berlin: Springer-Verlag, 2007.

Beauchamp, Tom L., and James F. Childress. *Principles of Biomedical Ethics*. 8th ed. Oxford: Oxford University Press, 2019.

Bellovin, Steven N. "Frank Miller: Inventor of the One-Time Pad." *Cryptologia* 35, no. 3 (2011): 203–222.

Bennett, Charles H., and Gilles Brassard. "Quantum Cryptography: Public Key Distribution and Coin Tossing." *Theoretical Computer Science* 560 (2014): 7–11. Originally published in *Proceedings of the International Conference on Computers, Systems and Signal Processing*, 175–179. Washington, DC: IEEE Computer Society, 1984.

Berkeley, Roy. *A Spy's London*. Barnsley, UK: Pen and Sword Military, 2014.

Bernstein, Daniel J., and Tanja Lange. "Post-Quantum Cryptography." *Nature* 549, no. 7671 (2017): 188–194.

Blake, Ian, Gadiel Seroussi, and Nigel Smart. *Advances in Elliptic Curve Cryptography*. Cambridge: Cambridge University Press, 2005.

Blake, Ian, Gadiel Seroussi, and Nigel Smart. *Elliptic Curves in Cryptography*. Cambridge: Cambridge University Press, 1999.

Bogdanov, Dan, Liina Kamm, Baldur Kubo, Reimo Rebane, Ville Sokk, and Riivo Talviste. "Students and Taxes: A Privacy-Preserving Study Using Secure Computation." *Proceedings on Privacy Enhancing Technologies* 3 (2016): 117–135.

Bohannon, John. "Breach of Trust." *Science* 347, no. 6221 (2015): 495–497.

Boneh, Dan. "The Decision Diffie-Hellman Problem." In *Algorithmic Number Theory, Third International Symposium, ANTS-III*, edited by Joe P. Buhler, 48–63. Berlin: Springer-Verlag, 1998.

Bruggeman, Tom, and Tom Gush. "Nice Cubic Polynomials for Curve Sketching." *Mathematics Magazine* 53, no. 4 (1980): 233–234.

Castryck, Wouter, and Thomas Decru. "An Efficient Key Recovery Attack on SIDH (Preliminary Version)." Cryptology ePrint Archive, Paper 2022/975, 2022. https://eprint.iacr.org/2022/975.

Checkoway, Stephen, Matthew Fredrikson, Ruben Niederhagen, Adam Everspaugh, Matthew Green, Tanja Lange, Thomas Ristenpart, Daniel J. Bernstein, Jake Maskiewicz, and Hovav Shacham. "On the Practical Exploitability of Dual EC in TLS Implementations." In *Proceedings of the 23rd USENIX Conference on Security Symposium*, 319–335. San Diego, CA: USENIX Association, 2014.

Churchill, David. "The Spectacle of Security: Lock-Picking Competitions and the Security Industry in Mid-Victorian Britain." *History Workshop Journal* 80, no. 1 (September 2015): 52–74.

Cramer, Ronald, and Victor Shoup. "A Practical Public Key Cryptosystem Provably Secure against Adaptive Chosen Ciphertext Attack." In *Advances in*

Cryptology—CRYPTO '98, edited by Hugo Krawczyk, 13–25. Berlin: Springer-Verlag, 1998.

Daemen, Joan, and Vincent Rijmen. *The Design of Rijndael: AES—the Advanced Encryption Standard*. Secaucus, NJ: Springer-Verlag, 2002.

Damgård, Ivan. "A 'Proof-Reading' of Some Issues in Cryptography." In *Automata, Languages and Programming*, edited by Lars Arge, Christian Cachin, Tomasz Jurdziński, and Andrzej Tarlecki, 2–11. Berlin: Springer-Verlag, 2007.

Dickens, Charles. *The Posthumous Papers of the Pickwick Club*. 1836–1837. Reprint, London: Penguin Classics, 2003.

Diffie, Whitfield, and Martin E. Hellman. "New Directions in Cryptography." *IEEE Transactions on Information Theory* 22, no. 6 (1976): 644–654.

Du, Wenlian, and Mikhail J. Atallah. "Protocols for Secure Remote Database Access with Approximate Matching." In *E-Commerce Security and Privacy*, edited by Anup K. Ghosh, 87–111. Boston: Springer-Verlag, 2001. https://doi.org/10.1007/978-1-4615-1467-1_6.

DuPont, Quinn. "The Printing Press and Cryptography: Alberti and the Dawn of a Notational Epoch." In *A Material History of Medieval and Early Modern Ciphers*, edited by Katherine Ellison and Susan Kim. New York: Routledge, 2018.

Elgamal, Taher. "A Public Key Cryptosystem and a Signature Scheme Based on Discrete Logarithms." In *Proceedings of CRYPTO '84: Advances in Cryptology*, 10–18. Berlin: Springer-Verlag, 1985. Originally published in *IEEE Transactions on Information Theory* 31, no. 4 (1985): 469–472. https://doi.org/10.1109/TIT.1985.1057074.

Evard, Jean-Claude. "Polynomials Whose Roots and Critical Points Are Integers." July 14, 2004. https://arxiv.org/abs/math/0407256.

Even, Shimon, Oded Goldreich, and Abraham Lempel. "A Randomized Protocol for Signing Contracts." *Communications of the ACM* 28, no. 6 (June 1985): 637–647. https://doi.org/10.1145/3812.3818.

Feynman, Richard. *The Character of Physical Law*. 1965. With a foreword by Frank Wilczek. Cambridge, MA: MIT Press, 2017.

Glinert, Ed. *The London Compendium: A Street-by-Street Exploration of the Hidden Metropolis*. London: Allen Lane, 2003.

Grover, Lov K. "A Fast Quantum Mechanical Algorithm for Database Search." In *Proceedings of the Twenty-Eighth Annual ACM Symposium on Theory of Computing*,

212–219. New York: Association for Computing Machinery, 1996. https://doi
.org/10.1145/237814.237866.

Hankerson, Darrel, Alfred Menezes, and Scott Vanstone. *Guide to Elliptic Curve Cryptography*. Berlin: Springer-Verlag, 2004.

Hardy, G. H. *A Mathematician's Apology*. 1940. Canto ed. Cambridge: Cambridge University Press, 1992.

Hobbs, A. C. *Locks and Safes: The Construction of Locks*. Rev. ed. 1868. London: Virtue and Co., 1853.

Horn, Robert D. "Dickens and the Patent Bramah Lock." *Dickensian* 62, no. 349 (1966): 100–105.

Iliffe, Rob. *Newton: A Very Short Introduction*. Oxford: Oxford University Press, 2007.

Ion, Mihaela, Ben Kreuter, Erhan Nergiz, Sarvar Patel, Shobhit Saxena, Karn Seth, David Shanahan, and Moti Yung. "Private Intersection-Sum Protocol with Applications to Attributing Aggregate Ad Conversions." Cryptology ePrint Archive, Report 2017/738, 2017.

Joseph, David, Rafael Misoczki, Marc Manzano, Joe Tricot, Fernando Dominguez Pinuaga, Olivier Lacombe, Stefan Leichenauer, Jack Hidary, Phil Venables, and Royal Hansen. "Transitioning Organizations to Post-Quantum Cryptography." *Nature* 605, no. 7909 (2022): 237–243.

Kahn, David. *The Codebreakers: The Comprehensive History of Secret Communication from Ancient Times to the Internet*. Rev. ed. New York: Scribner, 1996.

Kastner, Jeffrey. "A. C. Hobbs and the Great Lock Controversy of 1851." *Cabinet* 22 (Summer 2006). https://www.cabinetmagazine.org/issues/22/kastner.php.

Katz, Jonathan, and Yehuda Lindell. *Introduction to Modern Cryptography*. 3rd ed. Boca Raton, FL: CRC Press, 2021.

Kelly, Thomas. "The Myth of the Skytale." *Cryptologia* 22, no. 3 (1998): 244–260.

Kerckhoffs, Auguste. "La Cryptographie Militaire, Première Partie." *Journal des Sciences Militaires* 9 (January 1883): 5–38.

Kerckhoffs, Auguste. "La Cryptographie Militaire, Seconde Partie." *Journal des Sciences Militaires* 9 (February 1883): 161–191.

Koblitz, Neal. "Elliptic Curve Cryptosystems." *Mathematics of Computation* 48, no. 117 (January 1987): 203–209.

Koblitz, Neal. "The Uneasy Relationship between Mathematics and Cryptography." *Notices of the American Mathematical Society* 54, no. 8 (2007): 972–979.

Koblitz, Neal, and Alfred Menezes. "The Brave New World of Bodacious Assumptions in Cryptography." *Notices of the American Mathematical Society* 57, no. 3 (2010): 357–365.

Kocher, Paul C. "Timing Attacks on Implementations of Diffie-Hellman, RSA, DSS, and Other Systems." In *Advances in Cryptology—CRYPTO '96*, edited by Neal Koblitz, 104–113. Berlin: Springer-Verlag, 1996.

Kocher, Paul, Joshua Jaffe, and Benjamin Jun. "Differential Power Analysis." In *Advances in Cryptology—CRYPTO '99*, edited by Michael Wiener, 388–397. Berlin: Springer-Verlag, 1999.

Krawczyk, Hugo. "Koblitz's Arguments Disingenuous." *Notices of the American Mathematical Society* 54, no. 11 (2007): 1455–1456.

Lapets, Andrei, Frederick Jansen, Kinan Dak Albab, Rawane Issa, Lucy Qin, Mayank Varia, and Azer Bestavros. "Accessible Privacy-Preserving Web-Based Data Analysis for Assessing and Addressing Economic Inequalities." In *Proceedings of the 1st ACM SIGCAS Conference on Computing and Sustainable Societies*. New York: Association for Computing Machinery, 2018. https://doi.org/10.1145/3209811.3212701.

Lieberman, Erez, Jean-Baptiste Michel, Joe Jackson, Tina Tang, and Martin A. Nowak. "Quantifying the Evolutionary Dynamics of Language." *Nature* 449, no. 7163 (2007): 713–716.

Lindell, Yehuda. "Secure Multiparty Computation." *Communications of the ACM* 64, no. 1 (December 2021): 86–96. https://doi.org/10.1145/3387108.

Link, David. "Resurrecting Bomba Kryptologiczna: Archaeology of Algorithmic Artefacts, I." *Cryptologia* 33, no. 2 (2009): 166–182.

Lipton, Richard J., and Kenneth W. Regan. *Introduction to Quantum Algorithms via Linear Algebra*. 2nd ed. Cambridge, MA: MIT Press, 2021.

Mayzner, Mark S., and M. E. Tresselt. "Tables of Single-Letter and Digram Frequency Counts for Various Word-Length and Letter-Position Combinations." *Psychonomic Monograph Supplements* 1, no. 2 (1965): 13–32.

Miller, A. Ray. "The Cryptographic Mathematics of Enigma." *Cryptologia* 19, no. 1 (1995): 65–80.

Miller, Victor S. "Use of Elliptic Curves in Cryptography." In *Advances in Cryptology—CRYPTO '85 Proceedings*, edited by Hugh C. Williams, 417–426. Berlin: Springer-Verlag, 1986.

Moriarty, Kathleen, Burt Kaliski, Jakob Jonsson, and Andreas Rusch. "PKCS #1: RSA Cryptography Specifications Version 2.2." Request for Comments 8017, RFC Editor, November 2016. https://doi.org/10.17487/RFC8017.

Naor, Moni, and Adi Shamir. "Visual Cryptography." In *Advances in Cryptology—EUROCRYPT'94*, edited by Alfredo De Santis, 1–12. Berlin: Springer-Verlag, 1995.

National Institute of Standards and Technology (NIST). "Announcing Development of a Federal Information Processing Standard for Advanced Encryption Standard." *Federal Register* 62, no. 1 (1997): 93.

National Institute of Standards and Technology (NIST). "Announcing Development of Federal Information Processing Standard (FIPS) 180-2, Secure Hash Standard; a Revision of FIPS 180-1." *Federal Register* 67, no. 165 (2002): 54786–54787.

National Institute of Standards and Technology (NIST). "Announcing Development of Federal Information Processing Standard (FIPS) 180-4, Secure Hash Standard (SHS); a Revision of FIPS 180-3." *Federal Register* 77, no. 44 (2012): 13294–13295.

National Institute of Standards and Technology (NIST). "Announcing the ADVANCED ENCRYPTION STANDARD (AES)." Federal Information Processing Standards Publication 197. November 26, 2001.

Nielsen, Michael A., and Isaac L. Chuang. *Quantum Computation and Quantum Information*. 10th ann. ed. Cambridge: Cambridge University Press, 2010.

Peckam, Robert. *Fear: An Alternative History of the World*. London: Profile Books, 2013.

Pinkas, Benny, Mike Rosulek, Ni Trieu, and Avishay Yanai. "SpOT-Light: Lightweight Private Set Intersection from Sparse OT Extension." In *Advances in Cryptology—CRYPTO 2019*, edited by Alexandra Boldyreva and Daniele Micciancio, 401–431. Cham, Switz.: Springer International Publishing, 2019.

Pinkas, Benny, Thomas Schneider, and Michael Zohner. "Scalable Private Set Intersection Based on OT Extension." *ACM Transactions on Privacy and Security* 21, no. 2 (January 2018): 1–35. https://doi.org/10.1145/3154794.

Pinker, Steven. *The Better Angels of Our Nature: Why Violence Has Declined*. New York: Viking Penguin, 2011.

Preskill, John. "Quantum Computing 40 Years Later." 2023. https://arxiv.org /abs/2106.10522.

Rabin, Michael O. "How to Exchange Secrets with Oblivious Transfer." Aiken Computation Lab, Harvard University, 1981.

Ratcliff, Rebecca A. "How Statistics Led the Germans to Believe Enigma Secure and Why They Were Wrong: Neglecting the Practical Mathematics of Cipher Machines." *Cryptologia* 27, no. 2 (2003): 119–131.

Regalado, Antonio. "Cryptographers Have an Ethics Problem." *MIT Technology Review*, September 13, 2013. https://www.technologyreview.com/2013/09/13 /15059/cryptographers-have-an-ethics-problem/.

Rescorla, Eric. "The Transport Layer Security (TLS) Protocol Version 1.3." Request for Comments 8446, RFC Editor, August 2018. https://doi.org/10.17 487/RFC8446.

Rieffel, Eleanor, and Wolfgang Polak. *Quantum Computing: A Gentle Introduction*. Cambridge, MA: MIT Press, 2011.

Rivest, Ron L., Adi Shamir, and Leonard Adleman. "A Method for Obtaining Digital Signatures and Public-Key Cryptosystems." *Communications of the ACM* 21, no. 2 (February 1978): 120–126.

Rogaway, Phillip. "The Moral Character of Cryptographic Work." Cryptology ePrint Archive, Paper 2015/1162, 2015. https://eprint.iacr.org/2015/1162.

Scarani, Valerio, and Christian Kurtsiefer. "The Black Paper of Quantum Cryptography: Real Implementation Problems." *Theoretical Computer Science* 560 (2014): 27–32. https://doi.org/10.1016/j.tcs.2014.09.015.

Schlicke, Paul. *Oxford Reader's Companion to Dickens*. Oxford: Oxford University Press, 1999.

Shamir, Adi. "How to Share a Secret." *Communications of the ACM* 22, no. 11 (November 1979): 612–613. https://doi.org/10.1145/359168.359176.

Shannon, Claude E. "Communication Theory of Secrecy Systems." *Bell System Technical System* 28, no. 4 (1949): 656–715.

Shor, Peter W. "Algorithms for Quantum Computation: Discrete Logarithms and Factoring." In *Proceedings of the 35th Annual Symposium on Foundations of Computer Science*, 124–134. Washington, DC: IEEE Computer Society, 1994. https://doi.org/10.1109/SFCS.1994.365700.

Shor, Peter W. "Polynomial-Time Algorithms for Prime Factorization and Discrete Logarithms on a Quantum Computer." *SIAM Journal on Computing* 26, no. 5 (October 1997): 1484–1509.

Singh, Simon. *The Code Book: The Secret History of Codes and Code-Breaking*. London: Fourth Estate, 2002.

Trabesinger, Andreas. "Quantum Leaps, Bit by Bit." *Nature* 543, no. 7646 (2017): S2–S3.

von Neumann, John. "Various Techniques Used in Connection with Random Digits." In *Monte Carlo Method*, vol. 12, edited by A. S. Householder, G. E. Forsythe, and H. H. Germond. Washington, DC: National Bureau of Standards, US Government Printing Office, 1951.

Washington, Lawrence C. *Elliptic Curves: Number Theory and Cryptography*. Boca Raton, FL: CRC Press, 2008.

Webster, A. F., and S. E. Tavares. "On the Design of S-Boxes." In *Advances in Cryptology—CRYPTO '85 Proceedings*, edited by Hugh C. Williams, 523–534. Berlin: Springer-Verlag, 1986.

Wigderson, Avi. "Brief History of the Foundations of Cryptography." *Notices of the American Mathematical Society* 55, no. 1 (2008): 6–7.

Williams, Andy. "Advertising and Fiction in the *Pickwick Papers*." *Victorian Literature and Culture* 38, no. 2 (2010): 319–335. https://doi.org/10.1017/S106015031000001X.

Young, A., and Moti Yung. "Cryptovirology: Extortion-Based Security Threats and Countermeasures." In *Proceedings 1996 IEEE Symposium on Security and Privacy*, 129–140. https://doi.org/10.1109/SECPRI.1996.502676.

Young, Adam L., and Moti Yung. "Cryptovirology: The Birth, Neglect, and Explosion of Ransomware." *Communications of the ACM* 60, no. 7 (June 2017): 24–26. https://doi.org/10.1145/3097347.

FURTHER READING

Aaronson, Scott. *Quantum Computing since Democritus*. Cambridge: Cambridge University Press, 2013.

Anderson, Ross. *Security Engineering: A Guide to Building Dependable Distributed Systems*. 3rd ed. Indianapolis: John Wiley and Sons, 2020.

Aumasson, Jean-Philippe. *Serious Cryptography: A Practical Introduction to Modern Encryption*. San Francisco: No Starch Press, 2018.

Bauer, Friedrich L. *Decrypted Secrets: Methods and Maxims of Cryptology*. 4th ed. Berlin: Springer-Verlag, 2007.

Delfs, Hans, and Helmut Knebl. *Introduction to Cryptography: Principles and Applications*. 3rd ed. Heidelberg: Springer-Verlag, 2015.

Hodges, Andrew. *Alan Turing: The Enigma*. New York: Simon and Schuster, 1983.

Hoffstein, Jeffrey, Jill Pipher, and Joseph H. Silverman. *An Introduction to Mathematical Cryptography*. 2nd ed. New York: Springer-Verlag, 2014.

Holden, Joshua. *The Mathematics of Secrets: Cryptography from Caesar Ciphers to Digital Encryption*. Princeton, NJ: Princeton University Press, 2017.

Kahn, David. *The Codebreakers: The Comprehensive History of Secret Communication from Ancient Times to the Internet*. Rev. ed. New York: Scribner, 1996.

Katz, Jonathan, and Yehuda Lindell. *Introduction to Modern Cryptography*. 3rd ed. Boca Raton, FL: CRC Press, 2021.

Klein, Philip N. *A Cryptography Primer: Secrets and Promises*. Cambridge: Cambridge University Press, 2014.

Lipton, Richard J., and Kenneth W. Regan. *Introduction to Quantum Algorithms via Linear Algebra*. 2nd ed. Cambridge, MA: MIT Press, 2021.

Martin, Keith M. *Everyday Cryptography: Fundamental Principles and Applications*. 2nd ed. Oxford: Oxford University Press, 2017.

Mitani, Masaaki, Shinichi Sato, Idero Hinoki, and Verte Corp. *The Manga Guide to Cryptography*. San Francisco: No Starch Press, 2018.

Nielsen, Michael A., and Isaac L. Chuang. *Quantum Computation and Quantum Information*. 10th ann. ed. Cambridge: Cambridge University Press, 2010.

Paar, Christof, and Jan Pelzl. *Understanding Cryptography: A Textbook for Students and Practitioners*. Heidelberg: Springer-Verlag, 2010.

Piper, Fred, and Sean Murphy. *Cryptography: A Very Short Introduction*. Oxford: Oxford University Press, 2002.

Rieffel, Eleanor, and Wolfgang Polak. *Quantum Computing: A Gentle Introduction*. Cambridge, MA: MIT Press, 2011.

Schneier, Bruce. *Secrets and Lies: Digital Security in a Networked World*. 15th ann. ed. Hoboken, NJ: John Wiley and Sons, Inc., 2015.

Singh, Simon. *The Code Book: The Secret History of Codes and Code-Breaking*. London: Fourth Estate, 2002.

Smart, Nigel P. *Cryptography Made Simple*. Heidelberg: Springer-Verlag, 2016.

INDEX

PANOS LOURIDAS is Professor in the Department of Management Science and Technology at Athens University of Economics and Business. He is the author of *Real-World Algorithms: A Beginner's Guide* and *Algorithms* (Essential Knowledge Series), both published by MIT Press and translated into several languages worldwide. His research interests include software engineering, algorithmic applications, applied cryptography, and applied machine learning.